Paper
Science
Toys

Richard E. Churchill

Illustrated by James Michaels

 Sterling Publishing Co., Inc.   New York

For Eric—who knows more about things scientific in a minute than I do in a week—and willingly explains them as he has always done.

Edited by Timothy Nolan

Library of Congress Cataloging-in-Publication Data

Churchill, E. Richard (Elmer Richard)
  Paper science toys / by E. Richard Churchill.
      p.   cm.
  Includes index.
  Summary: Introduces scientific principles through toys made of paper, cardboard, and household items.
    1. Paper toy making—Juvenile literature. 2. Educational toys—Juvenile literature. [1. Paper toy making. 2 Educational toys. 3. Toy making. 4. Handicraft. 5. Science.]   I. Title.
  TT174.5.P3C478   1990
  745.592—dc20   90-9891
                                                       CIP
                                                       AC

10 9 8 7 6 5 4 3 2 1

Copyright © 1990 by E. Richard Churchill
Published by Sterling Publishing Company, Inc.
387 Park Avenue South, New York, N.Y. 10016
Distributed in Canada by Sterling Publishing
c/o Canadian Manda Group, P.O. Box 920, Station U
Toronto, Ontario, Canada M8Z 5P9
Distributed in Great Britain and Europe by Cassell PLC
Villiers House, 41/47 Strand, London WC2N 5JE, England
Distributed in Australia by Capricorn Ltd.
P.O Box 665, Lane Cove, NSW 2066
Manufactured in the United States of America

Sterling ISBN 0-8069-5834-0

Contents

Introduction

All the toys in this book can be made from paper or cardboard and other things you find around the house, like drinking straws or cardboard tubes.

All these toys work because of science. They are all based on scientific fact. Sometimes that may be easy to see, but other times it may be a bit hard to figure out. When this happens check the Lab Notes, and you'll find out why something works the way it does.

Now let's see what we can make and learn!

METRIC EQUIVALENCY CHART

MM—MILLIMETRES   CM—CENTIMETRES

INCHES TO MILLIMETRES AND CENTIMETRES

INCHES	MM	CM	INCHES	CM	INCHES	CM
⅛	3	0.3	9	22.9	30	76.2
¼	6	0.6	10	25.4	31	78.7
⅜	10	1.0	11	27.9	32	81.3
½	13	1.3	12	30.5	33	83.8
⅝	16	1.6	13	33.0	34	86.4
¾	19	1.9	14	35.6	35	88.9
⅞	22	2.2	15	38.1	36	91.4
1	25	2.5	16	40.6	37	94.0
1¼	32	3.2	17	43.2	38	96.5
1½	38	3.8	18	45.7	39	99.1
1¾	44	4.4	19	48.3	40	101.6
2	51	5.1	20	50.8	41	104.1
2½	64	6.4	21	53.3	42	106.7
3	76	7.6	22	55.9	43	109.2
3½	89	8.9	23	58.4	44	111.8
4	102	10.2	24	61.0	45	114.3
4½	114	11.4	25	63.5	46	116.8
5	127	12.7	26	66.0	47	119.4
6	152	15.2	27	68.6	48	121.9
7	178	17.8	28	71.1	49	124.5
8	203	20.3	29	73.7	50	127.0

· 1 ·
Sound Waves

Each and every time we hear a sound it is because sound waves have carried the sound into our ear. These toys will all depend on sound waves to make them work.

> ### LAB NOTES
>
> **Sound Wave.** Vibration or rapid movement sets air in motion. This creates the sound wave. Sound also travels through liquids and solids. Place your ear on one end of your desk and lightly tap your fingers on the other end. Now lift your ear and lightly tap your finger again. The sound was louder when your ear was on the table because sound travels better (and sometimes faster) through other substances than it does through the air.

Straw Horn

A paper drinking draw or a plastic straw is great for your straw horn.

Flatten the end of the straw as in Illus. 1. Don't smash it down so flat that it won't ever open up again, just push it down. If it's a plastic straw, just pinch it.

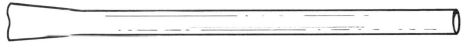

Illus. 1

With your scissors cut off a bit of both sides of the flattened end. These cuts should be about ¾-inch long. Remember to cut at an angle. Illus. 2 shows how.

Illus. 2

To use your straw horn, put the cut end into your mouth. Don't worry if it pulls apart. Be sure your lips are around the round, uncut part of the straw.

Now blow. You should be able to produce a horn sound which your parents won't love. If you don't get a sound, remove the straw horn and keep the cut ends together with your tongue. Now try blowing again.

If you still don't get a sound it may be because the ends are too stiff. Press the two cut ends together and try again. This time it'll work for sure.

Try touching the end of the straw with the tip of your tongue as you are blowing. Feel the straw vibrating? This vibration is creating the sound.

Now let's experiment. Trim the end of the straw just a bit so it looks like Illus. 3.

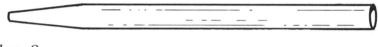

Illus. 3

Now blow the horn. You have changed the horn's tone! This is because the different shape of the loose ends causes them to vibrate differently than before.

Now cut off about an inch or so from the end of the straw not in your mouth. What happens to the tone now?

Use a strip of transparent tape to attach another straw to the end of your musical straw horn. Illus. 4 shows how. What happens to the straw's tone now?

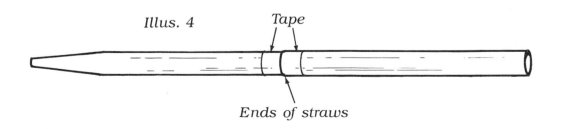

Illus. 4   *Tape*

Ends of straws

Two-Tone Straw

Try another experiment with a straw. Hold the straw so one end is against your lower lip as in Illus. 5. Now blow across the open end of the straw. Keep your lips fairly close together as you blow.

Illus. 5

Try covering the bottom end with your finger as in Illus. 6. Blow again. What has happened to the tone? The tone you hear from the closed straw is an octave lower than the tone from the straw when its bottom end is left open. Check the sound again by opening and closing the bottom of the straw.

Now cut a couple of inches from one end of the straw and open and close it again.

Because the straw's shorter, you start with a different tone. But when you close the straw's open end, the tone still changes an octave.

Finally, tape another straw to the end of the straw you are using. Now what happens to the tone? Does it change an octave when you cover the open end?

Illus. 6

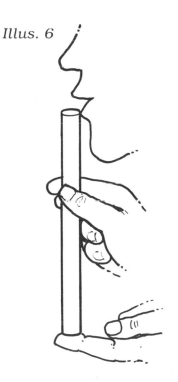

9

LAB NOTES

Octave. An octave is eight notes higher or lower than an original note.

Sound Wave Transfer Tube (and Cone)

We hear sound waves rather than see them, but here's a project which will let you see the sound waves, too. It is also a great magic trick.

You need a cardboard tube about 2 feet long. The rolls used to mail posters or the ones from inside wrapping paper will do the job. You can even make one from cereal box material. Just be sure to tape or glue the loose end tightly so no air can escape from it.

Now we need a paper cone. Take a piece of notebook paper, and roll it up, starting at an angle so the opening at one end is small and the other end is wide. The small end of your paper cone should be about ¼-inch across. The big end should be big enough to slip over the end of your cardboard tube.

Tape the paper cone together once you have it rolled to the right size; then slip the big end over the cardboard tube and tape it tightly into place. Don't worry if the cone gets a bit bent out of shape at the open end. Illus. 7 shows the project thus far.

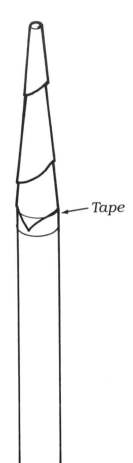

← Tape

Illus. 7

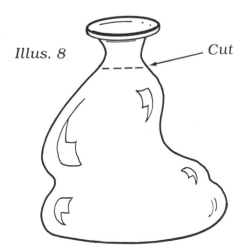

Illus. 8   — Cut

10

To finish our Sound Wave Transfer Tube (and Cone) (sounds impressive, doesn't it) you need a balloon. Blow it up to stretch the material; then cut off the neck of the balloon as in Illus. 8.

Stretch the balloon carefully over the end of the tube so it forms a tight layer over the opening. This thin layer will vibrate when it has to.

Now cut a very narrow strip of paper, about 4 inches long and 1/16-inch wide. Use a tiny bit of tape to fasten one end of the strip to a straw or pencil as in Illus. 9.

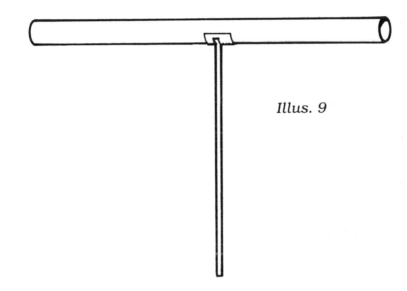

Illus. 9

Next, rest the ends of the straw or pencil on two boxes, glasses, books, or whatever is handy. Illus. 10 shows how.

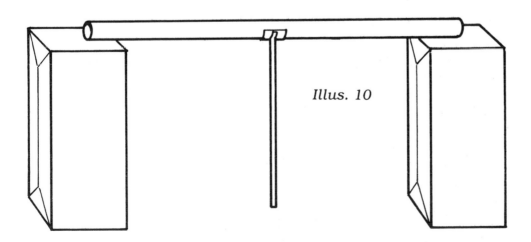

Illus. 10

11

Place the tube and cone on a table or desk so the balloon end extends into space a few inches. Set the paper strip and its holders right next to the opening in the cone and close enough to the strip so it almost (but not quite) touches the cone. Illus. 11 shows how.

Illus. 11

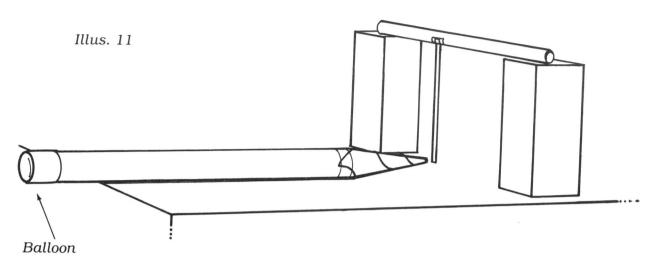

Balloon

To test the tube hold it with one hand, and with one finger of the other hand push in on the balloon. Let it spring back out and push it in again. As you do this watch the strip of paper. It will move away from the end of the cone. Since you are not touching the paper or blowing on it, anyone watching will think it is magic.

Now try clapping your hands right next to the balloon. Watch the strip of paper closely. It should move very slightly. Try having someone shout at the balloon. Any loud noise should make the paper at the end of the cone move.

LAB NOTES

Sound Waves. When the balloon moves it also causes the air inside the tube and cone to move. This moves the paper strip.

When you pushed the balloon with your finger, you caused the air inside the tube to move. But when you clapped or shouted or made some other loud noise, nothing touched the balloon except the sound waves the loud noise created.

Oat Carton Telephone

For this telephone you need a piece of string 20 feet long and two round oat cartons. If you don't have oat cartons handy, then two round salt cartons will work.

Remove the lids from the cartons, but don't throw them away (you will need them later).

Poke a small hole in the center of one carton's bottom as in Illus. 12. The end of a ball point pen works fine for making this hole.

Illus. 12

Hole

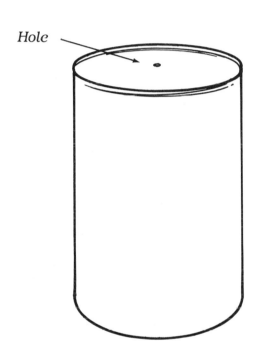

Push one end of the string through the hole. This string is your "phone line." Be sure to start the string through the bottom so it comes out inside the carton. Use the tip of the pen to push the string through the hole. Don't make the hole any larger than necessary.

Reach into the carton and use your fingernails to get hold of the tiny bit of string which comes through the hole. Pull it through the bottom and out the other end far enough so you can tie a large knot in the string's end. Illus. 13 shows how.

13

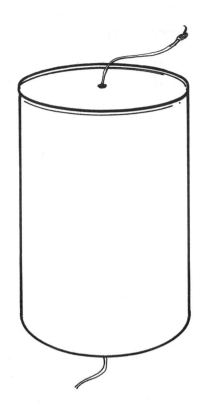

Illus. 13

Once you have tied the knot, pull the main part of the string slowly and firmly until the knot rests against the bottom of the oat carton.

Do the same thing with the second carton and the other end of the string, and your telephone is ready.

Stretch the string to full length between the two cartons. Pull it as taut as you can without ripping the knotted string out of the bottom of a carton. Illus. 14 shows the carton and string telephone in use.

Illus. 14

While one person places the open end of the oat carton over his or her ear, the other speaks directly into the other carton. The speaker should hold the open carton end right against his or her face. This helps contain the sound waves and directs them towards the bottom of the carton, which must vibrate.

The listener may find it easier to hear if he or she plugs the ear that is not inside the carton by covering it with a free hand.

Be sure the string is taut and does not touch anything between the two cartons. Talk and listen. This telephone really works. However, it will not work around corners because once the string touches an object it ruins the vibration.

See how far apart you and a friend can stand and still hear; then see how loudly and how softly you can speak and still be understood at the other end of the line.

If you rip the bottom of an oat carton, mend it with transparent tape. If the bottom gets too torn, glue or tape one of the tops you saved into place, and within a few minutes you have a brand new telephone.

LAB NOTES

Octaves and Vibrations. When vibrating air changes the tone by an octave, this means the air is vibrating twice as fast as before. Therefore, the air vibrates twice as fast in the open straw as in the closed one.

Also, the shorter the column of air, the higher the sound it makes, because air vibrates faster in a short straw than in a longer one. This is why the pipes in a church pipe organ are different sizes. The small pipes make high sounds and the thick, tall pipes create the deep bass sounds.

Telephone Lines. The sound waves from your voice cause the bottom of the carton to vibrate. This caused the taut string to vibrate. Naturally the vibration carried by the string causes the second oat carton bottom to vibrate, and that makes the sound the listener hears.

Goose Horn

This vibrating noisemaker may be called a goose horn because it sounds like a goose, or, because only someone silly as a goose would enjoy the sound it makes. Take your pick.

A file card makes a perfect goose horn. A 3 × 5-inch or a 4 × 6-inch card will do the job. If you don't have a file card, any piece of stiff paper will work (notebook paper is usually not stiff enough to do a good job).

Illus. 15 shows two shaded areas to be cut away. The tab between the shaded areas should be about ⅜-inch square.

Illus. 15

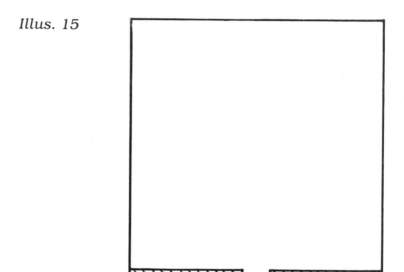

Roll the goose horn into a hollow tube as in Illus. 16. Use a bit of tape to keep it from unrolling.

Illus. 16

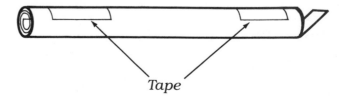

Tape

Fold the tab up so it covers the open center of the rolled tube. Be sure to roll the tube small enough so that this tab completely covers the opening. Place the end without the little tab in your mouth and gently suck in. You should be rewarded by a weird sound as the tab vibrates against the end of the horn. If not, suck a little harder or softer. If the tab does not pull up against the tube, push it into place with your finger and try again.

Once you discover the right combination, experiment with little bursts of pulled in air and longer pulls; then, for variety, reverse the goose horn so the tab is inside your mouth (don't get it wet). Blow gently; then a little harder. See what kind of sound you get.

Tube Kazoo

The tube from a roll of paper towels can be turned into a kazoo in a minute.

Cut a piece of wax paper big enough to cover one open end of the tube, with enough left over to wrap down onto the sides of the tube. Fit the wax paper over the end; then hold the paper in place with a rubber band as in Illus. 17.

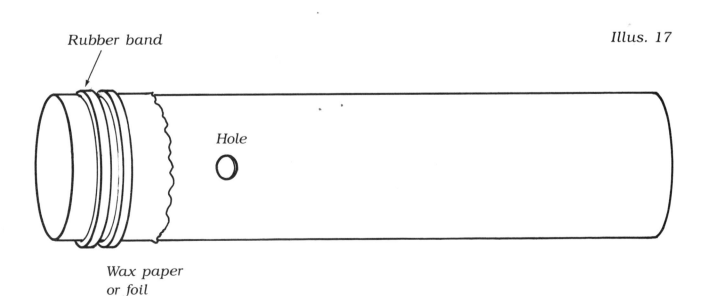

Rubber band

Illus. 17

Hole

Wax paper
or foil

Use a pen point or something else sharp and make a hole in the tube about 1½ inches from the covered end.

To make your kazoo do what kazoos do best, press the open end around your mouth and start humming (don't blow). If all goes as it should the wax paper will vibrate and you can make your Tube Kazoo hum a tune along with you.

To give your tube kazoo a different look and sound, use a piece of kitchen foil instead of wax paper. Be sure to tear off a piece large enough so it extends back over the hole in the side of the tube. Stretch it good and tight over the end of the tube, but don't press it down over the hole in the side. Put the rubber band in place and make sure a corner of the foil covers the hole in the kazoo's side, but be certain this corner of foil is loose and free to vibrate. Now try your new kazoo.

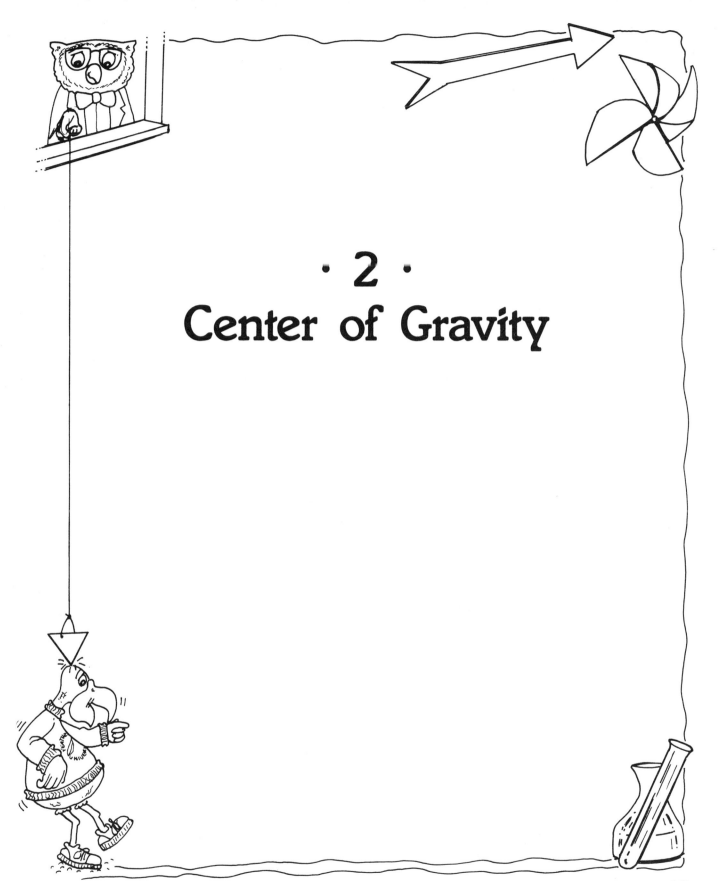

· 2 ·
Center of Gravity

The Amazing Tube

First we need a tube before it can become amazing. Roll a sheet of notebook paper into a hollow tube just big enough to hold a pencil inside. This is easier if you roll the paper around the pencil.

Remove the pencil and tape the loose sides of the tube in three places with transparent tape. Illus. 18 shows the taped tube.

Open a paper clip as in Illus. 19. Place one end of the clip next to an end of the tube and use two or three wraps of tape to hold it in place.

Illus. 18

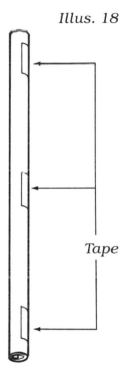

Tape

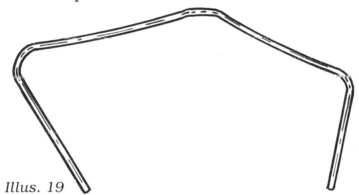

Illus. 19

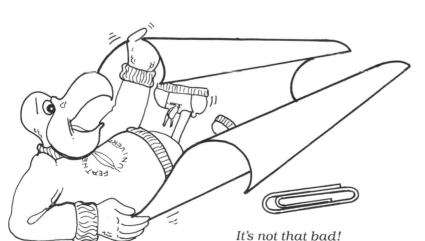

It's not that bad!

21

Extend one of your fingers and place the free end of the paper clip on the fingertip as in Illus. 20. Depending upon the angles in the bent paper clip, your amazing tube will hang in what may look like an impossible position.

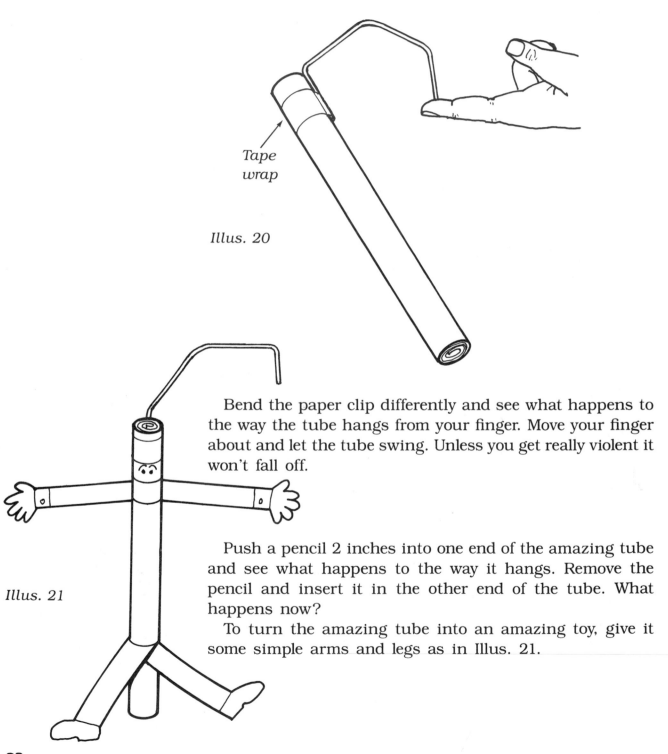

Tape wrap

Illus. 20

Bend the paper clip differently and see what happens to the way the tube hangs from your finger. Move your finger about and let the tube swing. Unless you get really violent it won't fall off.

Illus. 21

Push a pencil 2 inches into one end of the amazing tube and see what happens to the way it hangs. Remove the pencil and insert it in the other end of the tube. What happens now?

To turn the amazing tube into an amazing toy, give it some simple arms and legs as in Illus. 21.

Two strips of paper each 1 inch wide and about 6 inches long make great arms and legs. Fold the leg strip into the shape of an "L" as in Illus. 21. A bit of tape or glue holds the arms and legs in place after you have drawn or painted hands and feet.

You can really get into this and paint a face on it as well as coloring the body.

Try to balance it on the eraser end of a pencil, on the end of a ruler, on just about anything which isn't so slick the paper clip slides off.

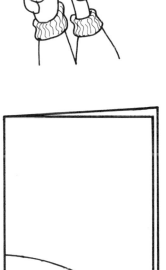

LAB NOTES

Tube's Center. If you look at your amazing tube you'll see that part of it is always on one side of the end of the paper clip resting on your finger, while part of the tube is on the other side of the clip's end.

Try to imagine a line extending straight down from the end of the paper clip. Exactly as much weight is on one side of that imaginary line as is on the other side.

Wing Walker

To make your Wing Walker you need a piece of cereal box material and a sheet of notebook paper for a pattern.

Fold the paper in half so it looks like Illus. 22, and draw in half of the Wing Walker. It does not have to look exactly like Illus. 22 but it should be fairly close. Notice that the wing tips extend down about 1½ inches lower than the end in the paper's fold.

Cut out the pattern while the paper is still folded. Unfold the pattern and trace it onto a piece of cereal box material. It should look pretty much like Illus. 23.

Illus. 22

Illus. 23

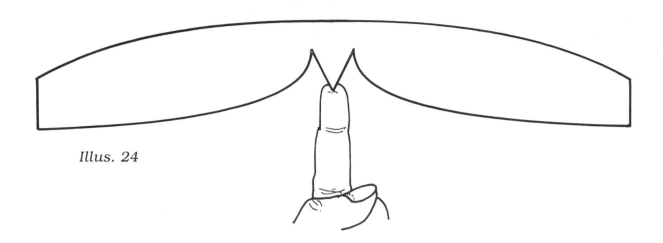

Set the center point on the end of your finger. Illus. 24 shows how. Did the Wing Walker slip right off your finger? Don't worry—just slip one paper clip onto the rear side of each wing tip. Illus. 25 shows how to position these clips.

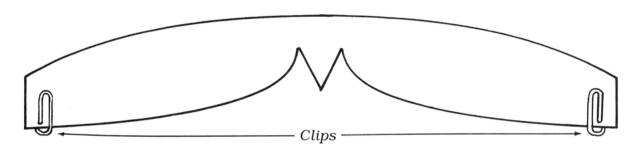

Clips

Illus. 25

Check the balance of your Wing Walker again. If it still does not balance, add two more paper clips. Add clips to the rear of the wing tips until your Wing Walker is in balance; then amaze and amuse others by showing them how your new toy seems to hang in a completely impossible manner from the end of your finger.

Make another Wing Walker with the wing tips further back. If you have a large enough piece of material, make a wider one as well.

Try some art work to make your Wing Walker really look great.

LAB NOTES

Center of Gravity. Think of the center of gravity as the one point in an object where all the weight is centered. At this point there is as much weight on any one side of the point as on any other.

Here's a tip when you try to balance objects such as the Amazing Tube or the Wing Walker. The point that you touch the object is called the point of support. Make certain the object's weight is concentrated below the point of support.

Plumb Bob

The Plumb Bob is a tool that shows the center of gravity at work.

Begin with half a sheet of fairly stiff paper. Notebook paper will work but heavier paper is better.

Roll the half sheet into a cone which is about 2 inches across at the large end and completely closed at the small end.

Use a dab of glue or a piece of transparent tape to hold the loose end of the cone in place. Illus. 26 shows where. Fold over the triangle of paper which is extending up from the big end of the cone.

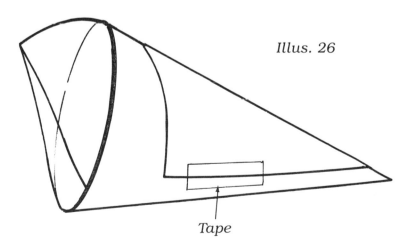

Illus. 26

Tape

A plumb bob for a plump bird!

To get the fold completely inside the cone you may have to make two folds. Fold down as much as you can without distorting the cone; then make a second fold to take care of any paper left sticking up out of the cone. Crease these folds well and you won't have to glue or tape the folded ends into place.

Illus. 27

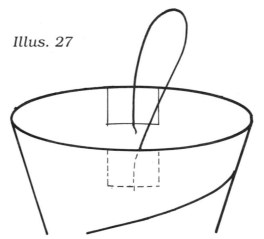

Now cut a piece of string about 5 inches long. Illus. 27 shows how to tape the ends of the string inside the open end of the cone. You can also cut the string a bit longer and punch holes in the sides of the cone; then tie the ends into the holes. Whichever way you choose, be absolutely certain to tape the string or punch the holes exactly opposite from one another.

Cut another piece of string 3 or 4 feet long and you're almost finished. Tie one end of this string around the cone string. Use a loose loop. Illus. 28 shows how. This allows your Plumb Bob to adjust itself so it always hangs vertically. Tie a loop in the other end of this string so you can hold the Plumb Bob around a finger or thumb. Drop a marble or a pebble into the cone and your Plumb Bob is ready for use.

Use it to check whether your door frames are straight up and down, and see how many tables and chairs are constructed with their legs not exactly vertical. You can even use the Plumb Bob to check the posture of your family members. Just make sure they don't start checking you for things other than posture if you and your Plumb Bob become a problem pair!

Illus. 28

LAB NOTES

Plumb Bobs. Construction workers have used plumb bobs for hundreds of years to keep buildings perfectly vertical. Though other instruments are now more commonly used, you may still see a plumb bob in use now and again.

This is a perfect example of using the pull of gravity in a meaningful manner. Think of the plumb bob's entire weight as centered at the point of the cone. This is its center of gravity.

Magic Balancing Act

This may give your friends a bit of a surprise.

Cut a circle from a piece of cereal box material. Three or 3½ inches across is ideal. If your circle isn't perfect don't worry about it. Lots of things in life work even if they aren't absolutely perfect.

Poke a hole in the center of the circle (just don't poke your finger or anything else!). Use a ball point pen or a wooden pencil. Push it far enough into the circle so 1½ inches of the pen sticks through. Things here look like Illus. 29.

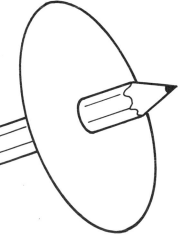

Illus. 29

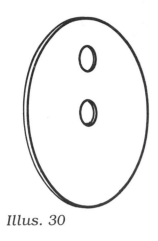

To make this a good magic act, pretend you are trying to balance the pencil and cardboard circle on the end of your finger. When it falls off, try to balance the pencil end on the side of your finger. When it won't balance again, move the cardboard closer to the pen or pencil point. Before everyone thinks you are a fool, tell them you'll just have to add more weight because heavy things are easier to balance.

Very carefully make a second hole between the center hole and one edge of the circle without ripping or bending the cardboard circle, as in Illus. 30.

Now roll a sheet of notebook paper into a tight tube and tape it together. Insert one end of the paper tube into the hole you just made in the circle, as in Illus. 31.

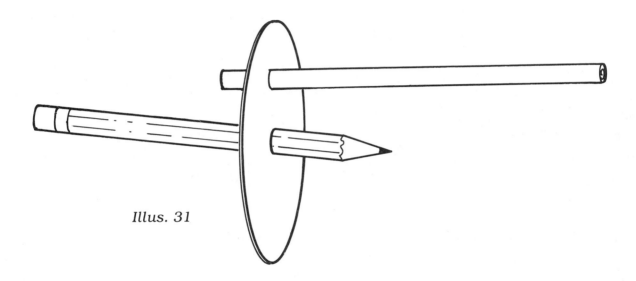

Illus. 31

By adding the paper tube on the side of the circle opposite most of the pen or pencil, you create a point of balance right at the tip of the pencil or pen.

If it still doesn't balance, adjust the pencil or pen by moving it slowly backwards or forwards until you can balance the toy on the side or end of your finger.

Three-Straw Toy

Hold three drinking straws together and press the ends down tightly as in Illus. 32. Wrap several inches of tape around the three straws. Keep the two outer straws in line with one another and hold the end of the middle straw

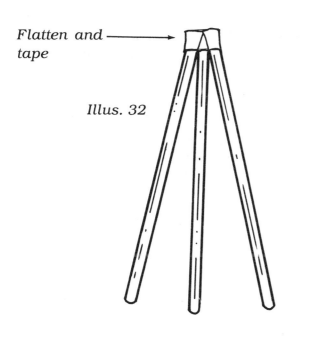

Flatten and tape →

Illus. 32

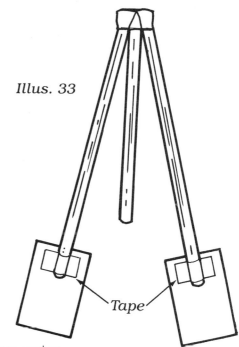

Illus. 33

Tape

higher while you tape them together. If you need an extra hand, lift the center straw while holding the others on the table top, after you have taped them. Once the center straw is raised so its loose end is about 2 inches higher than the others, use another piece of tape to hold things in place. When you are done, cut off about 2 inches of the middle straw.

Next, cut two rectangles out of cereal box material, 2 inches wide and 3 inches long.

Tape these pieces to the ends of the two long straws. Be sure to leave 1 inch of the straw on the end of each rectangle as seen in Illus. 33.

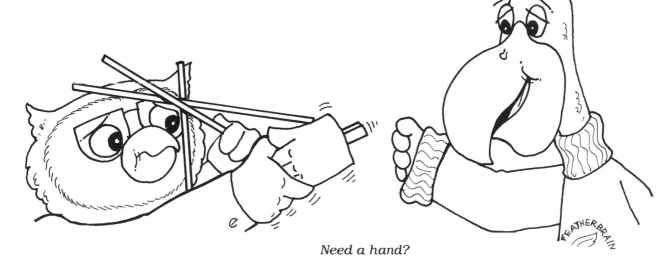

Need a hand?

Now balance your toy with the middle straw on the end of your finger. You may need to adjust the tape at the top a bit by moving the straws back and forth to get a perfect balance.

To make it even more impressive, push a straight pin through the end of the middle straw with the pin's head on the underside of the straw as in Illus. 34.

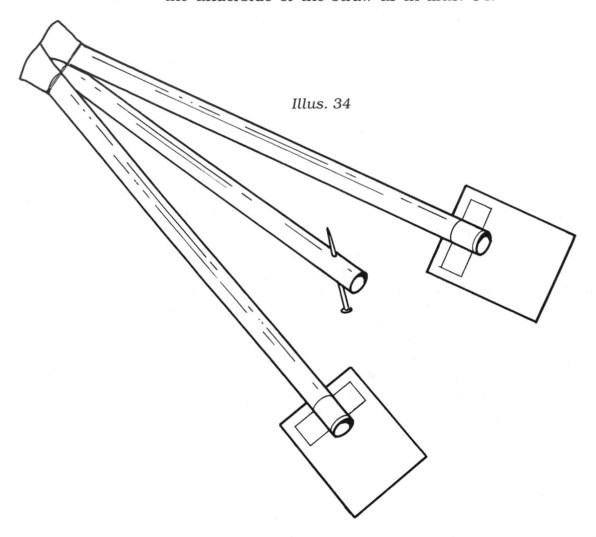

Illus. 34

Now balance the whole thing on the head of the pin atop your finger! Try balancing it on the tip of your finger with your finger pointing straight up; then carefully push the toy so it begins to spin slowly on the tip of your finger.

Why not build some incredible balancing toys of your own design? Just remember to keep the bulk of the toy's weight below the point of balance.

Leaning Cantilever

This stunt is fun to experiment with.

Start with a deck of cards. If you don't have a deck of cards, cut twelve or fifteen pieces of cereal box material so each piece is about 3 × 4 inches.

Place the deck at the edge of a table as in Illus. 35.

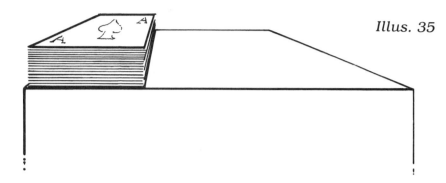

Illus. 35

Slide the top card out so it extends over the edge of the table 1 inch; then slide the next card out over the table edge. As the second card moves it will carry the top card with it.

This time slide the second card out about ⅝ inch. Slide the third card out ½ inch or less and continue in this manner. Illus. 36 gives you an idea how the cantilever looks.

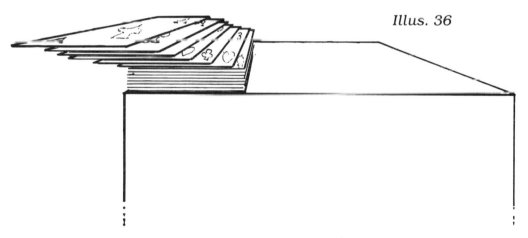

Illus. 36

Each time you slide a card out, make sure that the whole thing continues to balance. Eventually the top card will extend so far over the edge of the table that no part of it will actually be over the table.

See how far into space you can move the top card or whether it is possible for you to move more than one card out into space. A steady hand and a little patience will see you through.

Rock-a-Baby

This great toy can be as simple or as fancy as you want. Cut an oval like the one in Illus. 37 out of a file card or a piece of cereal box material. The one shown is about 4½ inches long and 2½ inches high.

Illus. 37

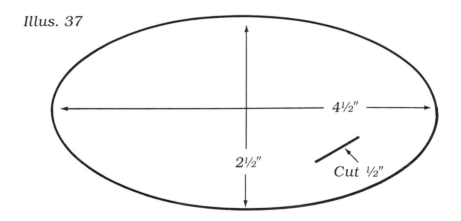

Carefully cut the slit shown in Illus. 37 ½-inch wide, and at a bit of an angle. Next, cut a piece of cereal box material ½-inch wide and 4 inches long. Round both ends so it looks like Illus. 38. Fold this narrow piece of material in the middle along the dotted line in Illus. 38. Slip one end of this narrow piece through the slit in the larger piece.

Now take a piece of wire 8 or 9 inches long. If you don't have a piece of wire, straighten out a couple of paper clips and splice them together by bending their ends around each other (you'll probably need a pair of pliers). If you do this, wrap several layers of tape tightly around the splice to help make it stronger.

Bend the wire into the shape as in Illus. 39. The short end at the angle bend should be about 1 inch long. Tape the bent end of the wire to your Rock-a-Baby as in Illus. 40.

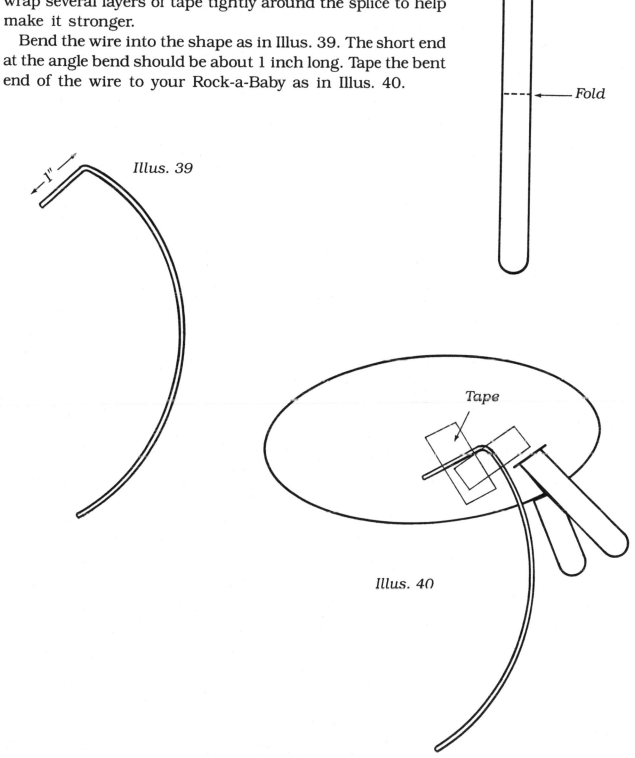

Illus. 38

Fold

Illus. 39

1"

Tape

Illus. 40

33

Cut a rectangle of cereal box material 1 × 3 inches, and attach it to the other end of the wire with a couple of paper clips. Illus. 41 shows the Rock-a-Baby ready for action.

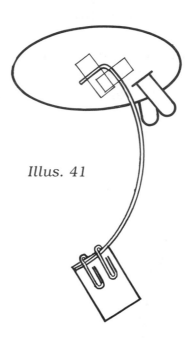

Illus. 41

Place the toy's legs in the palm of your hand and let go. If everything works as it should, the Rock-a-Baby will lean forwards but not fall off your hand.

If the toy won't balance, try bending the wire a bit to find a point of balance. If it still won't balance, add another paper clip or two to the weight at the bottom of the wire. If the legs slip apart, use a bit of tape to fasten them together so the ends of the legs are 1 inch from each other.

Try leaving the Rock-a-Baby hanging on the edge of a table or a shelf to startle and amuse anyone who passes by.

Paint or color the Rock-a-Baby, and give it front legs if you want. Make it in the shape of an animal if you wish.

LAB NOTES

Counterweight. The weight at the bottom of the Rock-a-Baby is sometimes known as a counterweight. This is because it counters or offsets the weight of the toy itself, which enables it to balance.

· 3 ·
Light and Sight

Visions on the Wall

Here's an interesting little toy.

On a piece of white paper draw the triangle as in Illus. 42. Make sure the lines are dark and fairly wide. The triangle should be about 1½ inches wide.

Illus. 42

Stare at the triangle for 30 seconds or so. Try not to blink (a few blinks won't spoil it).

After half a minute of staring, look away from the paper at a blank surface. Within 10 or 15 seconds a triangle should appear. However, it will be a bit different from the one you drew.

If you don't see a triangle on the wall, stare at the triangle for another 30 or 40 seconds and repeat the experiment.

Now, draw the circle as in Illus. 43. This time use red crayon. Make it 1 inch across.

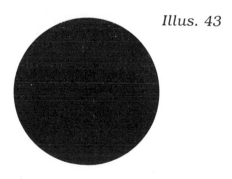

Illus. 43

This time stare at the drawing and at the wall. What color is the circle?

Move on to Illus. 44. Draw the rectangle with an orange crayon, and make it 1½ inches high and 2 inches long.

Illus. 44

Experiment with different drawings and colors. Try using two colors in the same drawing. Magic markers or colored pencils will do the job as long as the colors are good and dark.

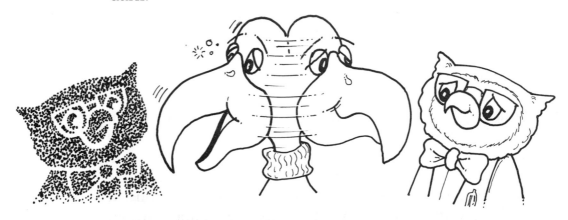

LAB NOTES

Afterimage. The scientific term for what you have just experienced is afterimage. An afterimage is sort of your mind's memory of what your eyes have just seen.

When you stare at the heavy, dark drawings, you imprint a picture of the image on the retina of your eye, which is at the back of the eyeball. This picture message is sent to the brain. When you look away from the actual drawing, the picture is strong enough for your eye and brain to remember it.

However, your eye and brain act like a camera when you see the afterimage on the wall. The vision you see is very much like a film negative.

Stroboscope

This fascinating paper toy takes just a few minutes to construct.

Draw a circle on a piece of white paper. Stiffer paper is better.

Locate the eight slits shown in Illus. 45. These should be evenly spaced. The best way to do this is to draw a line for each slit before cutting.

Illus. 45

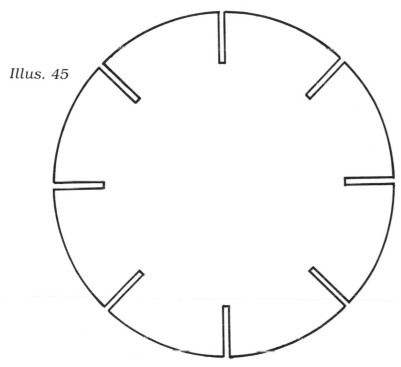

Draw two slits directly across from one another; then draw two more halfway between those you just drew. Now draw four more in between the first four. Steps A, B, and C in Illus. 46 show how to get the spacing just right.

Illus. 46

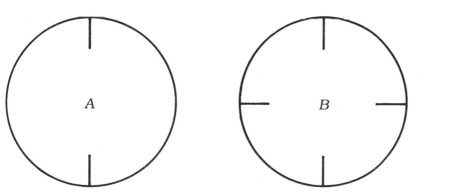

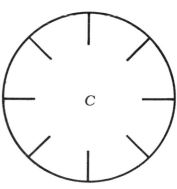

Cut out the eight slits, making each one about ⅛-inch wide and 1½ inches long.

Here's a hint in cutting these narrow slits. Cut along the two sides; then bend the narrow bit of paper upwards. Snip it off with the tip of your scissors.

Once the slits are cut, stick a straight pin through the center of the Stroboscope. Push the point of the pen into a pencil's eraser so it looks like Illus. 47.

Illus. 47

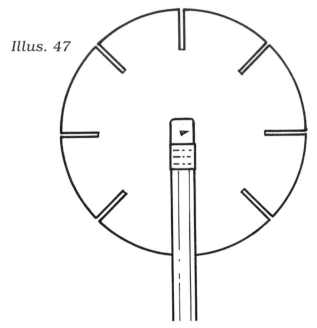

Take your Stroboscope to the nearest mirror. Hold it directly in front of you as you look into the mirror, as in Illus. 48. Look through one of the slits at your reflection. Now, with your free hand, spin the Stroboscope. Keep looking right through the slits into the mirror. Spin it faster and slower. A funny thing happens when you find the proper speed.

Illus. 48

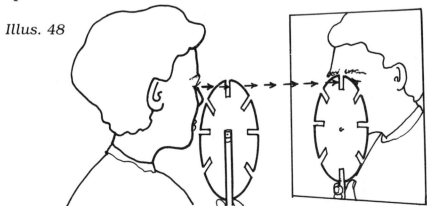

Suddenly you are looking at a Stroboscope in the mirror which is standing still. Your eye is looking through a slit which does not move.

By varying the Stroboscope's speed you can make the image in the mirror appear to move slowly the same way the circle is spinning or move slowly backwards. Experiment a bit and see this happen.

Let's try another experiment. Turn on a record turntable without a record on it. As the turntable revolves, look at it through your spinning Stroboscope. Focus on the outer edge of the turntable.

Try arranging several small pieces of paper on the turntable's outer edge. Pieces ½ × 1 inch are just about right. Space four of them equally and observe them through our Stroboscope. Add four more pieces and see what happens.

LAB NOTES

Stroboscope. The Stroboscope works because your eye is seeing a series of images evenly spaced. Each time your eye sees through the narrow slit in the spinning paper disk it takes a mental picture of what it sees. The after-image effect allows your brain to retain or remember that image.

Pin Hole Magnifier

Cut out a 2-inch square of white paper. With the point of a pin make a hole right in the center of the paper. You have just made a Pin Hole Magnifier like the one in Illus. 49.

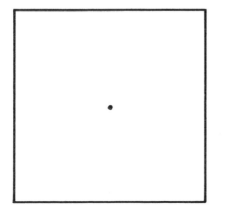

Illus. 49

But where is the glass? Everyone knows a magnifier has glass in it.

This one doesn't. To test it, hold the magnifier so the hole is about an inch above this page. Place your eye close enough to the hole so you can see through it (be sure there is enough light).

Find a book, magazine, or newspaper with smaller print. Check this with your Pin Hole Magnifier. You can move it back and forth a bit to find the perfect focus for you.

Now try your Pin Hole Magnifier on things other than printed words, like the blossom of a flower or a tiny hair on your arm.

Make a Pin Hole Magnifier with a slightly larger hole and see what happens.

LAB NOTES

Depth of Focus. The hole cannot magnify. Only a lens can do that. What happens is the tiny hole lets you position your eye quite close to the printed letters. Since you are only looking at a small portion, your depth of focus is increased. In other words, the smaller the hole in the paper the closer you can hold the printed word to your eye. Larger holes cause you to hold your eye a bit farther away in order to focus.

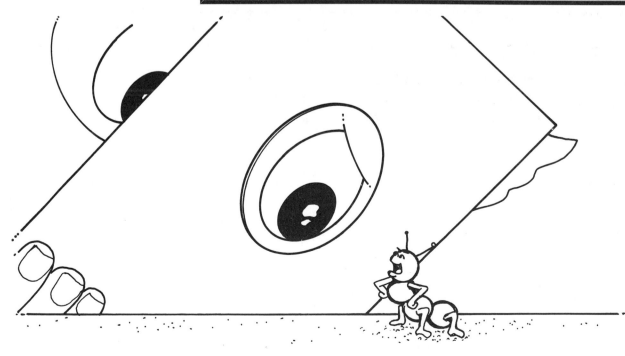

Primary Color Spinner

The three 'primary' colors are red, blue, and yellow. They are called primary because blends or mixtures of these three colors create all the other colors.

To make the spinner, cut a 4-inch circle of cereal box material, and color one third of it red, another third blue, and the final third yellow, as in Illus. 50. Next, punch two holes in the spinner. These holes are also in Illus. 50.

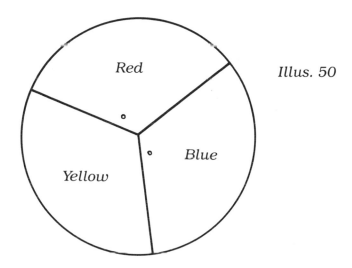

Illus. 50

Cut a piece of heavy string about 3 feet long to complete your spinner. Thread one end through one of the holes in the spinner and then back through the other. Tie the loose ends firmly together. Illus. 51 shows your completed spinner.

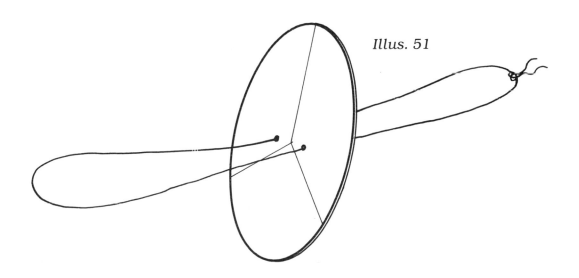

Illus. 51

To make your spinner do its thing, slip two fingers of each hand through the loops in the ends of the string. Twirl it around and around until the string is twisted for a dozen or so turns. Illus. 52 shows this.

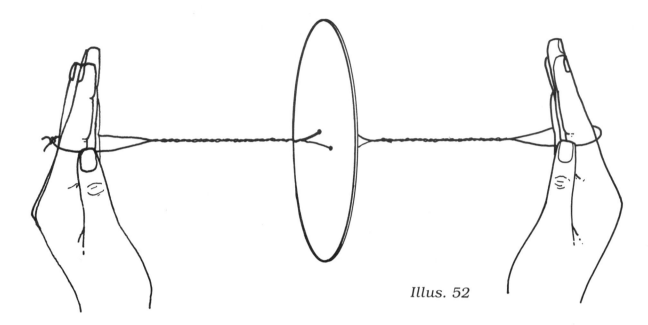

Illus. 52

Now, pull your hands apart firmly. As the string unwinds, the spinner will turn rapidly. When your hands are apart and the string is completely unwound, let the spinner's momentum keep it turning and retwist the string in the opposite direction. As this happens, allow your hands to move together so the string can turn and twist (this takes a bit of practice, so don't worry).

If the spinner lays over on its side, cut a small, round piece of cardboard and glue it to the center of the disc. Of course you'll have to punch holes in it and rethread the string.

Once you have the disc spinning properly, look at the colored side. What happened to the three colors? Why is the disc suddenly white or pale instead of brightly colored?

Your eye and brain see all three colors when the spinner is not moving. Once it begins to spin rapidly your eye becomes confused because the reflected colors are passing so rapidly it is impossible to register which color is flying by. Therefore, the three colors blend together and the result is white or a very light color.

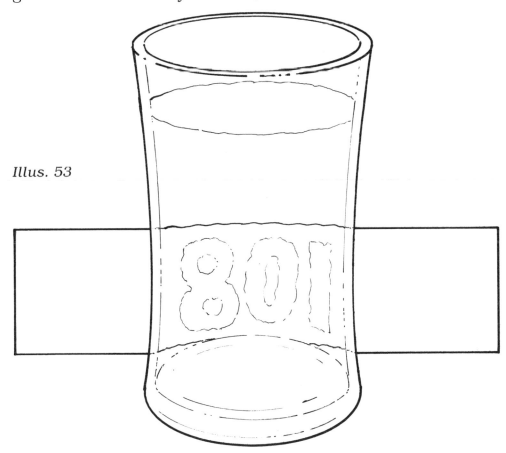

LAB NOTES

Light Rays. Light is made up of all the colors our eye can see. When the eye and brain tell us something is red or blue or any other color, this is because that object is reflecting only red or blue or some other light rays. It is absorbing or soaking up the light rays for other colors.

Magic Number

On a piece of white paper neatly write the number 108.

Fill a glass with water. Hold the card or piece of paper directly behind the glass so you are looking through the glass at the number you wrote, as in Illus. 53.

Illus. 53

Now look at the number through the glass of water. You may have to move the number around a bit so you can see it. The number you wrote was 108. What do you see through the glass of water?

The Appearing Dot

Cut a piece of white paper or lightweight cardboard about ½-inch square. Draw a dot in the center about ⅛-inch in diameter.

Pull off about 1½ inches of tape and form it into a hollow cylinder with the sticky side out. Overlap one end of the tape onto the other so it does not pull apart.

Press the piece of paper or cardboard onto one side of the sticky roll; then push the rest of the sticky tape into the bottom of a tea cup. Illus. 54 shows this.

Illus. 54

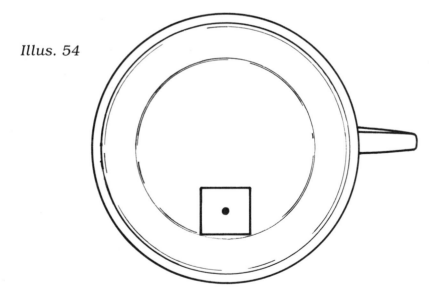

Now place the cup on a table or counter and stand so your line of vision lets you see over the edge of the cup into the bottom but so you can't see the paper or the dot. Illus. 55 shows how to set this up.

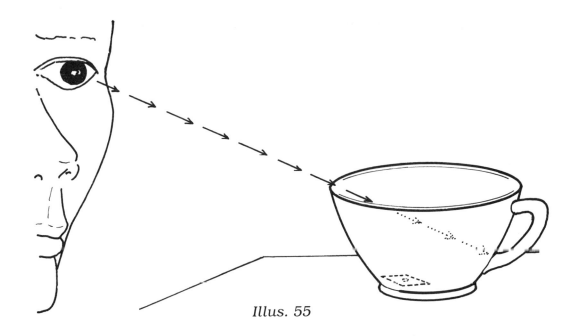

Illus. 55

Have a friend very slowly and gently begin to pour water into the cup. Meanwhile, continue to look over the rim of the cup. As the water level rises you are going to see something very strange indeed.

If you don't have a friend handy, set the cup in the sink under the faucet. Start the water running very slowly and stand back to watch what happens.

Obviously the tape did not let the dotted paper move. So why can you see the paper and finally the dot?

Light reflected from the paper and the dot bounces up out of the cup. This light reflects upwards through the water. When the light comes out of the water into the air it bends or changes direction just a little bit. The more water there is in the cup, the greater this change in direction. Actually, the water acts like a lens when it causes this bending or change in direction.

Try this experiment with something other than a dot on paper to see how it works.

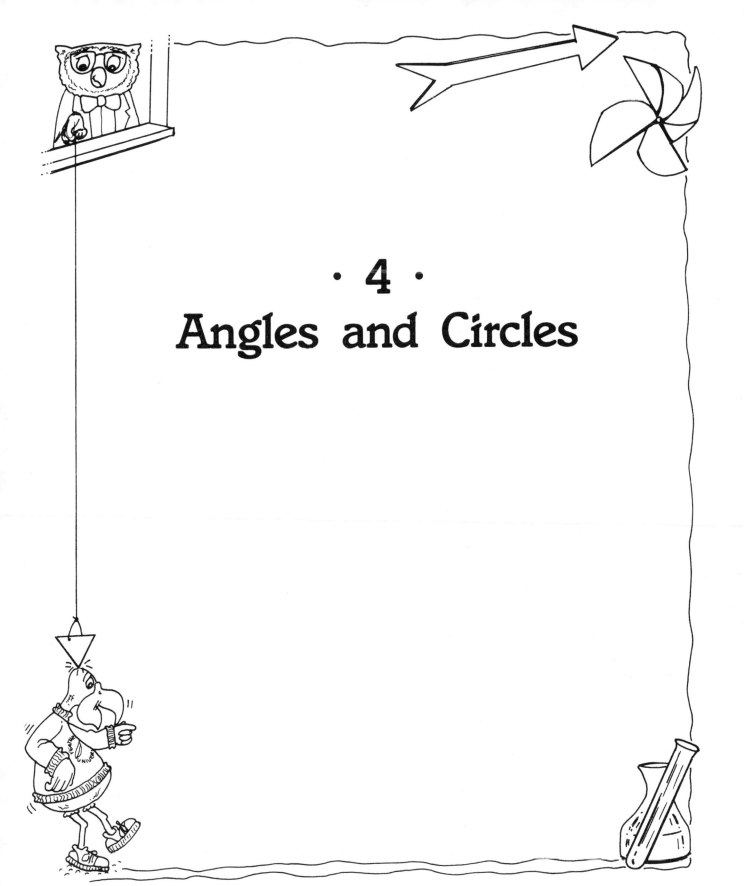

· 4 ·
Angles and Circles

Many pieces of scientific equipment use mathematical angles and circles in their construction. This shows the close connection between science and mathematics.

Giant Compass Arm

Cut a piece of cardboard about 1 inch wide and at least 13 inches long. This is going to become your Giant Compass Arm. Round the ends of the arm a bit as shown in Illus. 56 to make the project look professional.

About ½-inch from one end of the compass arm make a small hole. Be sure the hole is in the cardboard and not in your finger or the tabletop.

Measure 4 inches along the compass arm from the hole you just made. Mark this point with a dot. Continue along the compass arm, making a dot every inch along the entire distance of the compass arm. Illus. 56 shows how the compass arm appears.

Punch a small hole into each dot you measured. Be sure to hold the compass arm steady as you do this. You don't want it to bend. Label each of the small holes along the compass arm. Illus. 57 shows how to identify each hole with the distance it is from the first hole you made.

Illus. 57

| 4″ | 5″ | 6″ | 7″ | 8″ | 9″ |

Place a thumbtack or a round toothpick in the first hole you made. The tack or toothpick is the pivot point around which your compass arm will swing to draw large circles. A piece or two of tape over the head of the tack or tucked around the toothpick will help make sure your pivot point does not slip out when the compass arm is in use.

Place the pivot point at the center of your future circle. If you want to draw a circle 12 inches across, place the pencil point through the hole labeled six. This is because the circle has a radius of 6 inches.

Hold the pivot point steady. Rotate the compass arm in a complete circle, keeping the pencil or pen upright. Lift the compass arm and there is your 12-inch circle, ready for use.

Measuring Wheel

Cut out a circle of stiff cardboard, 3.82 inches across. Since it is a bit difficult to draw a circle exactly 3.82 inches in diameter, make your circle 3⁸⁄₁₀ inches across. This means the circle will have a radius of 1⁹⁄₁₀ inches. Take your time and measure carefully if you want the completed measuring wheel to measure exactly.

Once the circle is drawn and cut out, make a small hole in the center for the axle. Draw an arrow at one point along the outer rim of the circle as in Illus. 58.

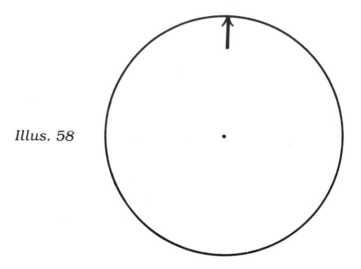

Illus. 58

Stand the circle on its edge. Position it so the arrow points right at the beginning of a ruler or yardstick as in Illus. 59.

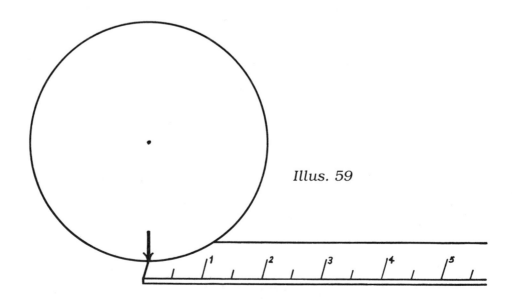

Illus. 59

Very slowly and carefully start turning the circle so it travels along the ruler. When you reach 1 inch, mark that point on the circle's circumference with a dot.

Continue turning the circle marking the outer rim every inch. When you have turned the circle one complete turn, the arrow you drew should be at the twelve inch mark.

Label each dot 1, 2, 3, etc., until you have moved all the way around the circle. Each time your measuring wheel makes one complete turn or revolution it will have traveled 12 inches of one foot.

Cut two strips of cereal box material. Each one should be 1 inch wide and about 12 inches long. Poke a small hole about ½-inch from one end in each strip. These two pieces will form the wheel's handle.

If you have a paper fastener, push it through one handle piece; then push it through the center of the measuring wheel and finally, through the second handle. You can also use a paper clip that is straightened a bit to get it through the three layers of material. Once through, fold it back against the handle. A piece of tape over the top of the clip on each handle helps hold things in place.

Take a look at Illus. 60. Finish the measuring wheel by wrapping a strip of tape around the ends of both handles to keep them firmly together. Now begin measuring things by running your wheel across or around them.

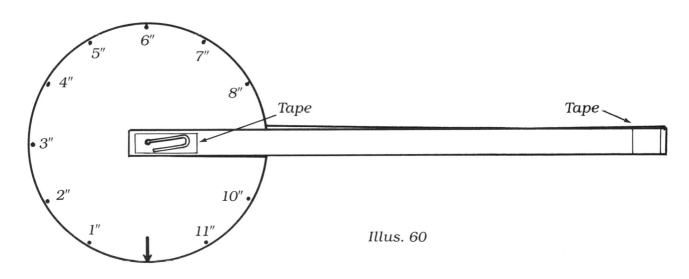

Illus. 60

To measure larger areas, you need a larger measuring wheel. Make this one 11.46 inches across. This is just a shade less than 11½ inches in diameter. A wheel this size gives you a circumference of 1 yard.

Draw a large arrow to show where the yard begins. Dots will locate each inch. At 12 and 24 inches make a small arrow to keep track of how far your wheel has turned.

Make the handles for this larger wheel longer than those for the first wheel. The second wheel should also be a bit wider, about 2 inches. If you don't have material long enough for the handle, splice two pieces together with tape or glue.

Code Wheels

Almost as soon as writing was invented people wanted to send messages that no one other than the sender and the receiver could read. Codes were the answer.

Draw a circle 5³⁄₁₆ inches in diameter on a piece of stiff material (5¼ inches is close enough). Cereal box cardboard or a piece of file folder is just fine. Light-colored red material is great since you are going to have to write on the cardboard.

Now you'll have to do some extremely careful measuring and marking. Every ⅝-inch write a letter of the alphabet all the way around the circumference or outer rim of this master code wheel. If you don't get the letters lined up perfectly you'll run into a whole bunch of trouble when it comes to writing messages in code.

Begin by marking the code wheel as shown in Illus. 61. Note that "A" and "N" are exactly across from each other. The two dots half way between "A" and "N" on either side of the wheel are each exactly one quarter of the way around the wheel.

"G" and "H" are exactly ⅝ inch apart, which means they are each ⁵⁄₁₆-inch from the dot separating them. The same thing is true for "T" and "U" across the wheel.

Now fill in the rest of the letters, making sure that they are all ⅝-inch apart. Illus. 62 shows this step with the first section complete. This is your master code wheel.

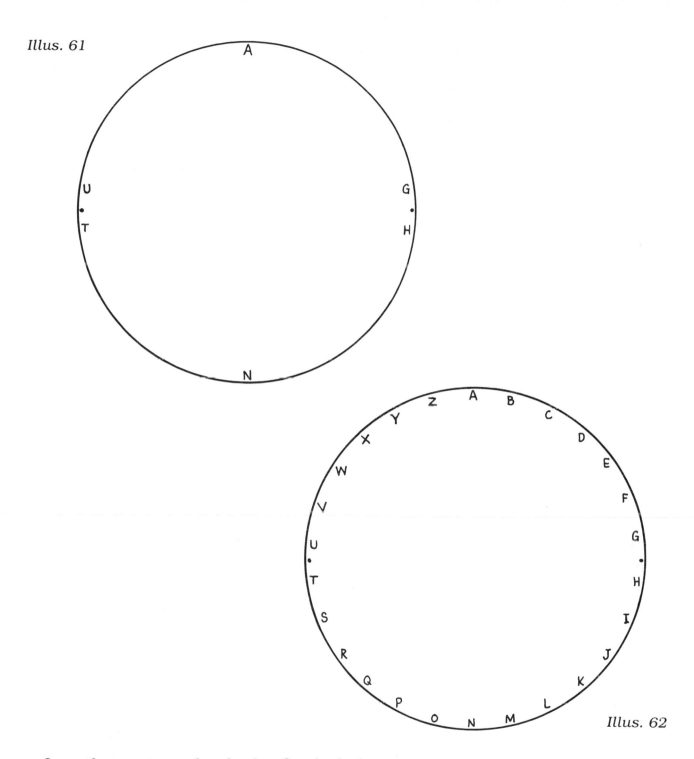

Illus. 61

Illus. 62

Once the master code wheel is finished, the rest is easy. Cut a circle 4 inches across from stiff paper of lightweight cardboard. This is the inner wheel and will have your code on it. Label this wheel I just so we know it is the code wheel (if you want to add more codes, make code wheels II, III, IV, and so on).

Place this inner code wheel on top of the master code wheel as in Illus. 63. Note the arrow at the top of the code wheel shown in the drawing. This arrow always points to the "A" in the master code wheel when the code wheel is in its basic position.

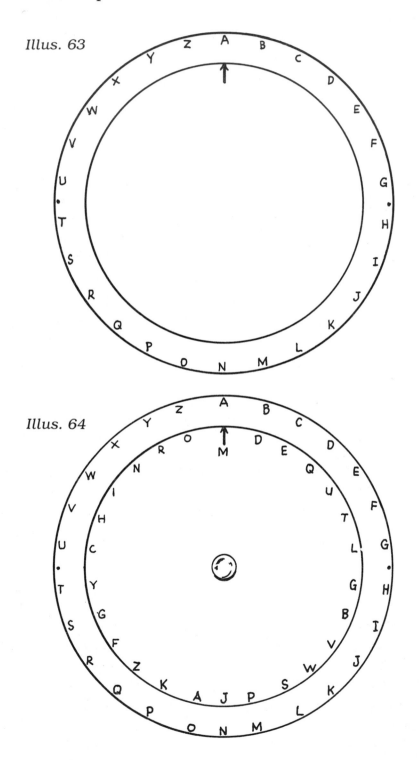

Illus. 63

Illus. 64

To build your first code, make sure the inner code wheel does not slip or slide around. Be certain each letter you write on the code wheel is lined up exactly with a letter on the master wheel.

Write the alphabet on the inner wheel, but write it in scrambled order. Mix up the letters all around the edge of the inner wheel. Illus. 64 shows the code in place. Once all twenty-six letters are spaced around the inner wheel, you are ready to write your first coded message.

Each time you want to write a letter, check to see what letter is beside it on the inner wheel. Write that letter in your coded message.

Say you need to write the word "BAG." As you can see in Illus. 64 "D" in the inner wheel is beside "B" on the master wheel. "M" is below "A" and "L" is beside "G". Therefore "BAG" becomes "DML" when you write the word in code.

It is obvious that the person receiving your message needs a pair of code wheels exactly like the ones you used in writing your message. Therefore you'll need to make the duplicates at the same time you construct the originals.

Now to get really tricky. Good international agents and military leaders know better than to use the same code day after day. You can change the code you just made by merely rotating the inner wheel. Instead of having the arrow point to "A," rotate it two places so it now points to "C". This changes every letter and gives you a completely new code.

To tell the person receiving the code you have changed codes, simply begin your messages I–2. This means you are using code wheel I but have rotated it two letters. Simple but extremely effective. Now "BAG" would be written "ORU".

To keep the inner wheel from slipping, push a thumb tack through the center of it and through the master wheel to keep them in place. A thick piece of cardboard under the two wheels keeps the point of the tack from scratching table tops and the like.

Try a Code Wheel in which numbers are substituted for letters. To be really confusing, pick random numbers from one to 100 to represent letters. Thus, 35 might stand for "A" and 76 could represent "B". There's no limit to the number of codes you can develop. And, of course, every inner code wheel can be used for twenty-six different codes by rotating it inside the master wheel.

A
B
C
D
E
F
G
H
I
J
K
L
M
N
O
P
Q
R
S
T
U
V
W
X
Y
Z

Illus. 65

Code Cylinders

Code cylinders work exactly the same as code wheels, but look entirely different.

Begin with a strip of lined notebook paper like the one in Illus. 65. As you can see, the alphabet appears in order. This means this is the master strip. Note there is about an inch of space beside each letter. Also note there is an inch or so of extra space at one end of the letter strip.

Illus. 66 shows how to overlap the letter strip to form the master cylinder. A bit of transparent tape or glue will hold the master cylinder in place.

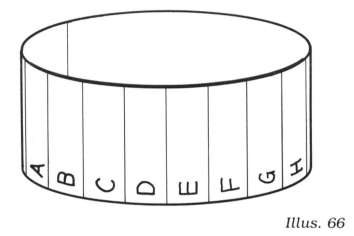

Illus. 66

Cut a second strip of lined notebook paper exactly like the one for the master strip except that about ½-inch less wide.

Mark the first letter with an arrow to show where to line up this code strip with the master strip. The arrow will always point at the letter "A" when the two pieces are lined up in basic position, just as with the Code Wheels.

Write the letters of the alphabet in random order with one letter per line on the inner strip. Wrap the code strip around the master strip so the arrow is lined up with the letter A. You may use tape or glue to make a cylinder of the inner strip just as you did for the master strip. Illus. 67 shows the inner strip in place on the master strip. You can also put a paper clip over the two cylinders to keep them from slipping while you are encoding or decoding.

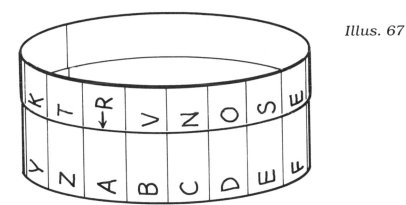

You can alter any code by moving the code strip to a new starting position. If you wish you can have a number of code strips. Just remember to label them I, II, III, etc. Feel free to use numbers instead of letters, as well.

Codes are lots of fun, especially when no one can tell what your messages say unless they have cylinders that match yours.

Hypsometer

How many times have you wondered how tall a flagpole or building was? A geometric measuring square will help you answer such a question.

This square is called a hypsometer, and it has been around since the Middle Ages. It is easy to construct and use. First, cut a 1-foot square of cardboard. Stiff cardboard from packing boxes is perfect (just be extremely careful when cutting it).

How tall is it?

Cereal box material will work as well as heavier cardboard if you cut two squares and glue them together. If you have to include a fold from the cereal box, turn one piece a quarter turn to keep the folds from coming on top of one another.

With your ruler or yardstick, mark the bottom edge of the square at 1-inch intervals, starting at the right edges. Illus. 68 shows this step.

Illus. 68

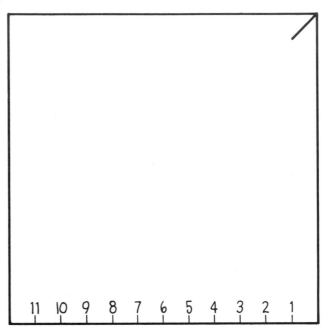

Look at the short cut in the upper right hand corner of the square in Illus. 68. Make this cut about ½-inch long and be sure it is made diagonally.

Next you need a plumb bob (page 25). Tie a large knot in the other end of the string, and slip the string into the cut. Pull on it until the knot comes right up against the back of the cardboard. Now your Hypsometer is ready for use.

Illus. 69 shows the square with the plumb bob attached. It also shows how to use the square. Hold the square in front of your face. The top edge of the square should be in a straight line from your eye to the upper edge of what you are measuring. Illus. 70 shows this.

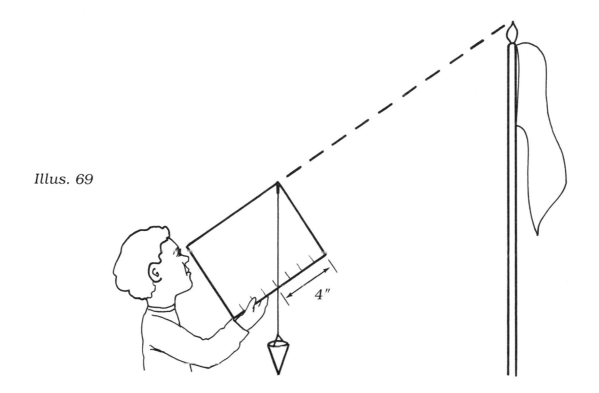

4″

Now check the plumb bob. How many inches back is the line hanging? Let's say it is 4 inches. Measure the distance from where you are standing to the bottom of the building, tree, or pole. If you have the large Measuring Wheel (page 52) handy, you will be exact. In this example let's assume it is 24 feet. Now measure the distance from the level of your eye to the ground. Again, let's say it's 4 feet.

Illus. 70

12′

4′

24′

Multiply the number of inches along the bottom of the square (4) by the distance in feet from the object to where you stood (24) and you get 96. Divide this number by 12 and you get 8. Add the height in feet (4) your eye is above the ground, and you get 12. So, if we sighted and measured correctly, the height of the object is 12 feet.

Here are a couple of hints to make things easier. Try to get the plumb bob's string right across one of the inch measurements. This will make multiplying easier.

It is helpful to have a partner to watch the plumb bob line and tell you exactly where it is.

When you divide by 12 you will often have a remainder. It may be easier to put the remainder in inches. Say you multiplied 5 and 15 and got 75. Dividing by 12 gives 6 remainder 3. You can consider this 6 feet and 3 inches or 6¼ feet. Either way, just add the height of your eye and you have the object's height.

> ## LAB NOTES
>
> **Geometry.** Two similar triangles are formed (one is the triangle at the bottom and front of the square when the plumb bob's string crosses it; the other is the ground, the object viewed, and the line of sight along the top of the square). The ratios of corresponding triangle sides are used to do the rest.

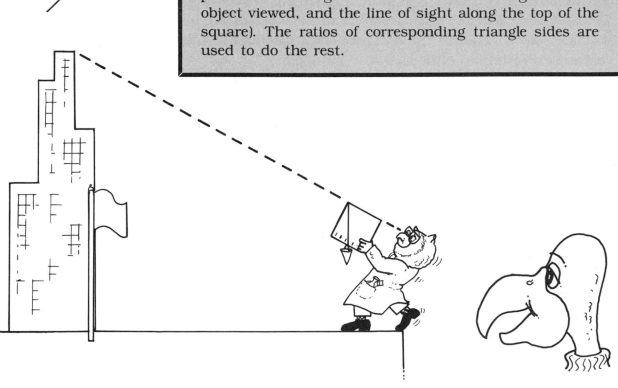

Pantograph

A pantograph is a simple little gadget which enables you to copy a simple drawing larger than the original.

Cereal box material will do nicely for your first pantograph, though after you make your first model you may decide to glue several layers together to make it stronger and stiffer.

Cut out four bars as shown in Illus. 71. Pay close attention to the total length of each piece.

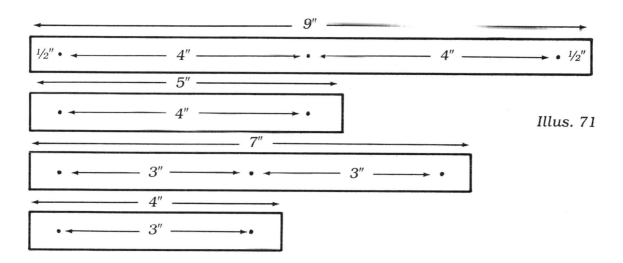

Illus. 71

Carefully poke small holes in each piece of material (it is a good idea to put some newspaper under each piece as you poke a hole through it). Make sure they are the exact distances apart as shown in Illus. 71. Each end hole is exactly ½-inch from the end of the bar of cardboard. Keep these holes small. You can enlarge them later if necessary.

When all the holes are made, round the end of each bar of cardboard. Illus. 72 shows the smallest piece with the holes punched and the ends rounded. Set these pieces aside for a minute.

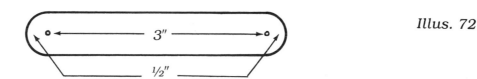

Illus. 72

Now you need a base for the pantograph. Cereal box material is just fine. Cut out a piece about 1 foot high and 1 foot or more wide. Carefully poke or punch the hole shown in Illus. 73.

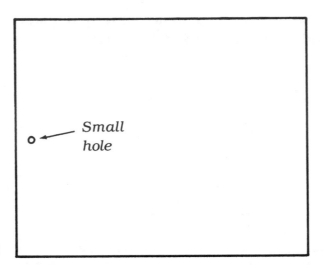

Small hole

Illus. 73

To assemble the pantograph, you need four paper fasteners or paper clips. If you don't have paper fasteners, just slip one end of the paper clip through the two pieces of materials you are joining together, and place a chunk of tape over the top of the clip and tape it down to the cardboard bar.

Illus. 74 shows how things go together.

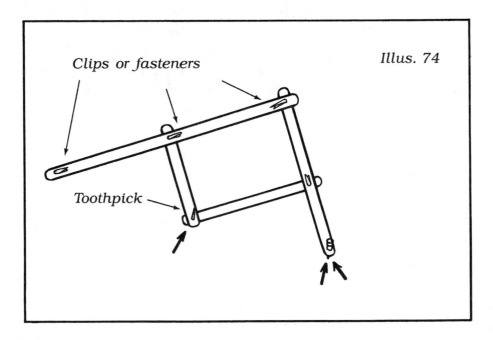

Clips or fasteners

Illus. 74

Toothpick

Note the longest bar has one end fastened to the base. Check to see that the bar below this one is parallel to it.

Push a round toothpick through the hole shown by the arrow in Illus. 74. This toothpick holds two bars together. It should stick through so that ½-inch or so protrudes below the bottom.

To finish the pantograph, press the point of a soft-leaded pencil, ball point pen, or nylon-tipped pen through the hole by the double arrow in Illus. 74. You may have to enlarge the hole to fit the pencil or pen point. It should stick through the bar about ½-inch.

Place a simple drawing under the toothpick. Slip a blank sheet of paper under the pen or pencil.

Carefully begin to trace the drawing with the point of the toothpick. The pen or pencil point will follow the movement of the toothpick except it will make a larger copy of the drawing.

You may need to steady the pen or pencil with your fingertip as in Illus. 75. Just make sure any pressure you apply is not so heavy it keeps the pen or pencil from moving freely.

Illus. 75

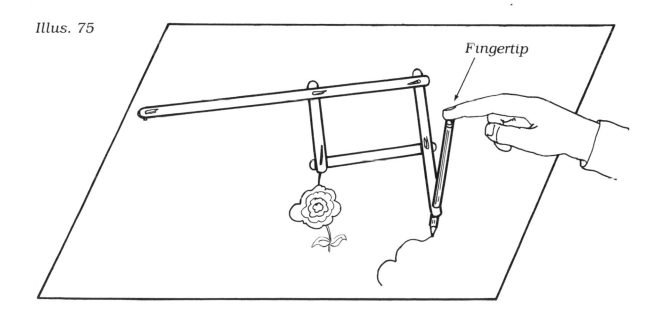

Fingertip

If the pantograph seems too limber, use double layers of cereal box material. Remember to remove the fasteners or clips before gluing the double pieces together.

By putting the toothpick in the pen hole and changing the pen to the toothpick's spot, you can make a pantograph which produces smaller drawings than the original.

Try changing the dimensions of the pantograph so it will enlarge or reduce more than this one. Remember that the two parts marked "A" in Illus. 76 must always be the same length between holes. The same is true for the two parts marked "B".

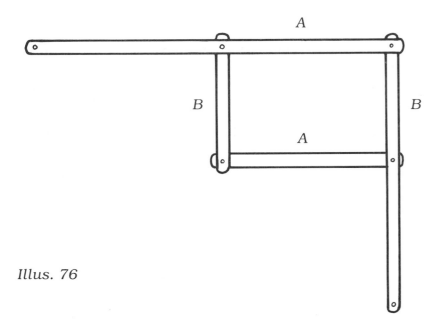

Illus. 76

LAB NOTES

Parallelogram. A pantograph works because the *A* bars and *B* bars are parallel to each other. These pairs of parallel bars form a parallelogram.

· 5 ·
Time and Direction

Sundial

Before people had watches and clocks, they still had to know what time it was. So they used the sun.

Begin with a piece of cardboard 8 or 9 inches square. Draw the two diagonal lines shown in Illus. 77. Where these lines cross is the center of the square. Use it for the center of a 7-inch circle.

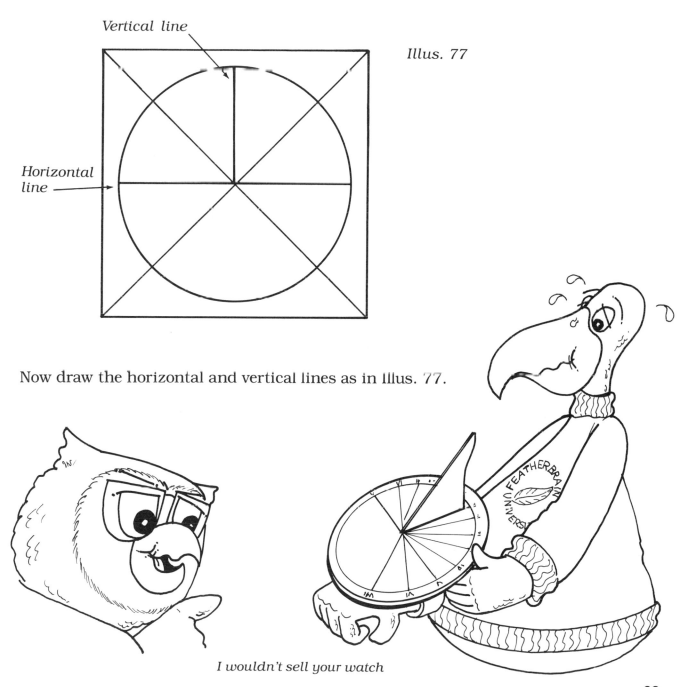

Vertical line

Illus. 77

Horizontal line

Now draw the horizontal and vertical lines as in Illus. 77.

I wouldn't sell your watch

Number both ends of the horizontal lines "6." Mark the top of the circle "12", and the diagonal lines mark "3" and "9," as in Illus. 78.

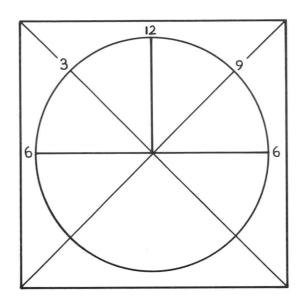

Illus. 78

Fill in the remaining hours, spacing them evenly along the rim of the circle between those numbers already filled in. When you finish you have the top half of the Sundial numbered from 6:00 in the morning until 6:00 in the evening.

On another piece of cardboard, draw the 3-inch-long horizontal line as in Illus. 79. Using a protractor, measure an angle which is equal to the latitude where you live (a protractor is the little half-circle device used to measure angles). You can find the latitude of your town or city on a map or atlas. It is the grid line which runs east and west.

In Illus. 79 the angle measured is 40°, so this Sundial will work for any city or town on that line (if you are a degree or two off, don't worry).

Illus. 79

8″

40°

|← 3″ →|

Once you have measured the angle, draw an 8-inch line from the right end of the small line as in Illus. 79. Draw the third side of the triangle to connect the other two lines as in Illus. 80. Also, add the tree tabs in Illus. 80. Each tab is 1 inch wide and ½-inch or so high. Cut this piece out and cut between tabs, as in Illus. 80.

Fold the outer tabs to the right and the one in the middle to the left and you are ready to mount this piece to the base of the Sundial. Use tape or glue to fasten it in place. The base should run right along the line from the dial's center to noon, with the end touching the circle at noon. This means there is ½-inch of space between the middle of the dial and the other end of the upright's base. Illus. 81 shows the finished Sundial.

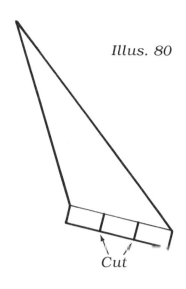

Illus. 80

Cut

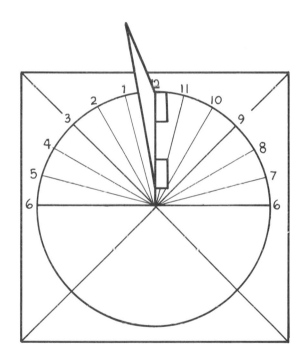

Illus. 81

Line it up with the sun so the base of the dial points north and the upright points south. The shadow cast by the upright should let you read the time from the numbers located on the upper half of the Sundial. Just remember to adjust for daylight saving time.

Obviously your Sundial won't work on cloudy, hazy days. If you are on daylight saving time, remember the time shown on the Sundial is sun time, not 'clock' time. Your Sundial will be off by one hour during daylight saving time.

Watch Compass

This project needs a watch with hands (digital watches won't work).

Cut a piece of cardboard 5 inches square. Right in the

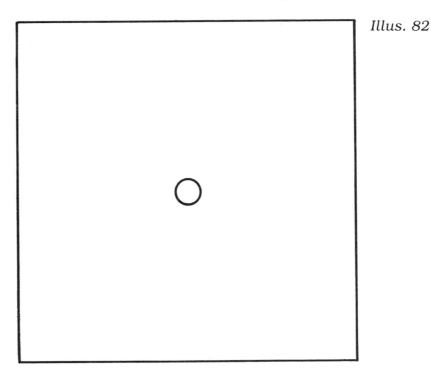

Illus. 82

middle make a hole just large enough for a drinking straw to slip through. Illus. 82 shows how.

Now make three 1-inch cuts in one end of the straw. Fold the sections back as in Illus. 83. If you don't have a drinking straw, just cut a 2-inch strip of notebook paper. Roll the paper into a tube, tape or glue the loose side, and make the cuts.

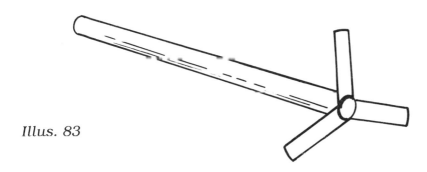

Illus. 83

Push the uncut end of the straw through the hole until the three spread parts rest against the bottom of the base. Tape them down tightly as in Illus. 84.

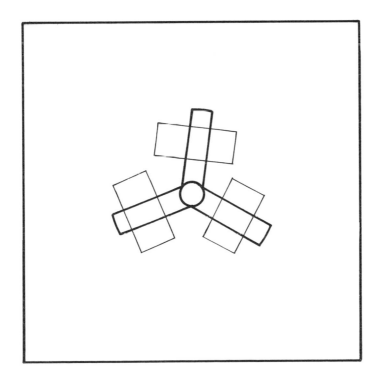

Illus. 84

Set the base upright so the straw extends vertically. Lay your watch against the base of the straw as in Illus. 85.

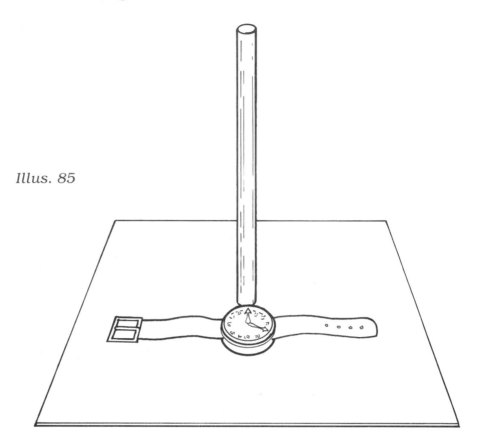

Illus. 85

The straw will create a shadow from the straw. Turn your watch so its hour hand is covered by the shadow. This means the hour hand is painted directly toward the sun.

South is halfway between the hour hand and the number 12 on the face of your watch. For example, the hour hand is on 10, and halfway between 10 and 12 is 11, then south is in the direction of the 11 on the watch face.

Remember daylight saving! If you are on daylight saving, south is halfway between the hour hand and 1 on the watch.

LAB NOTES

Direction Directions. If you live in Australia, keep in mind you use this method to find north instead of south.

Small Sundial

This Small Sundial can be folded up and carried in your pocket; just don't expect it to replace your watch!

A piece of stiff paper or the side from a manila folder is perfect for this sundial. Draw a 3-inch square in the center of the material. Locate the center of the square and draw a 1¾-inch circle inside the square as in Illus. 86.

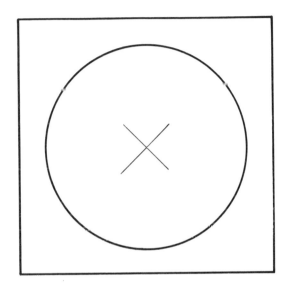

Illus. 86

Next, number the circumference of the circle from 1 to 12 as in Illus. 87. Make certain 6 is at the top and 12 at the bottom and the 3 and 9 are on the sides; then space the rest of the numbers evenly.

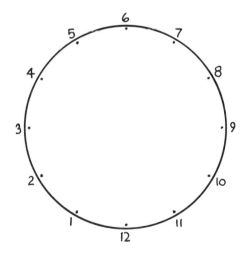

Illus. 87

Place a ruler through the center of the circle (which is also the square's center, naturally). Measure 1½ inches from the bottom of the square and place a dot at point "A" in Illus. 88; then draw a line 2 inches long from the center of the top of the square to point "B" in Illus. 88.

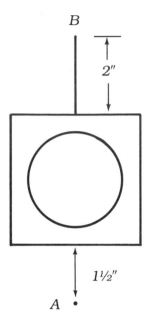

Illus. 88

B

2"

1½"

A •

Now draw another 2-inch line up from the corner.

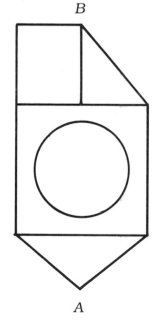

Illus. 89

B

A

76

Connect point "B" with the line you just drew; then connect "B" with the other corner. Now, connect point "A" with the two lower corners. Illus. 89 shows this.

Now take your latitude number and subtract it from 90 (if you live on a latitude of 40°, then take 40 from 90 and you get 50).

With your protractor, lay out a 50° angle from the lower left and right corners 2 inches to points "C" and "D," respectively.

Draw lines from points "C" and "D" to the remaining corners, as in Illus. 90.

Illus. 90

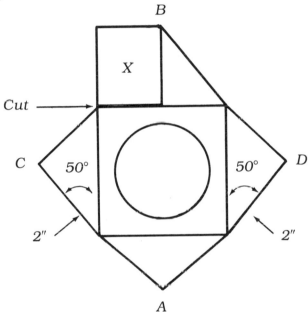

Cut out the sundial, and make the cut from corner shown in Illus. 90.

Now for some folding. Fold up point "A" and point "B"; then fold down point "C" and point "D" Finally fold the rectangle (marked "X" in Illus. 90) up along line "B".

Use a bit of tape to fasten this rectangle of material into place so its lower corner comes to the center of the folding sundial. Illus. 91 shows your finished sundial.

Illus. 91

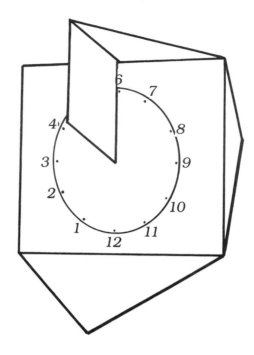

Be sure points "C" and "D" rest on a flat surface. Point "A" should face north. The face of the sundial is now at an angle.

Read the time from the shadow and remember that daylight saving time causes your sundial to be one hour off.

If you wish to carry your folding sundial along on a hike or camping trip, just loosen the tape and it will fold flat.

· 6 ·
Force and Motion

Force is energy applied to an object. Motion, obviously, is movement. Force can both cause motion and change the direction of motion.

Anything that moves needs some sort of force to make it move. The force can be a push or a pull. It can be gravity. Running water can also force motion.

Water Powered Boat

To build a Water Powered Boat you first need a hull. The best thing for the hull is a milk or juice carton (a half-gallon carton is best, but a quart will work just fine). Cut away one side of the carton as in Illus. 92. Be sure to cut away the side shown so the boat ends up with a pointed front or bow. Don't cut off too much material. The sides should remain pretty high.

Illus. 92

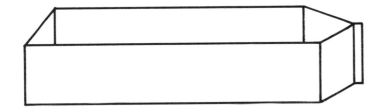

Make a hole just big enough for a drinking straw to go through in the rear or stern of the boat. Illus. 93 shows this.

Illus. 93

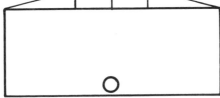

Now you need an engine. A soft drink cup is perfect, the larger, the better. Poke another hole for a drinking straw near the cup's bottom as in Illus. 94.

Illus. 94

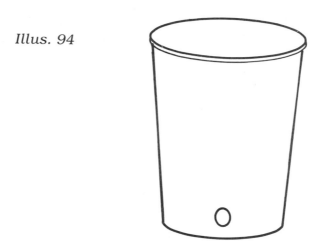

Now install a plastic drinking straw so one end sticks into the cup and the other end protrudes from the boat's stern as in Illus. 95.

Illus. 95

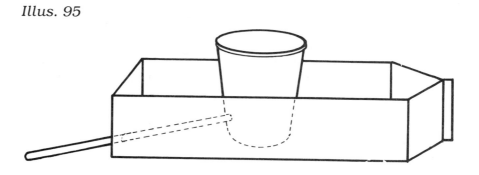

Be sure the end of the straw coming out the boat's stern is long enough so that it will extend under the surface of the water. If it isn't, join another straw or half a straw. To join the straws, cut two 1-inch slits in the end of one straw, and press the cut ends together so they overlap just a bit. This makes the end a little smaller so you can push it into the other straw.

Check your boat in the sink or bathtub. Don't fill it in; a couple of inches of water will do just fine.

Make sure the soft drink cup is in the middle of your boat. Fill the cup with water, and hold a finger over the end of the straw. Remove your finger, and the boat will move off across the sink or tub.

If you want to make a rudder for your boat, Illus. 96 shows a pattern for a simple design.

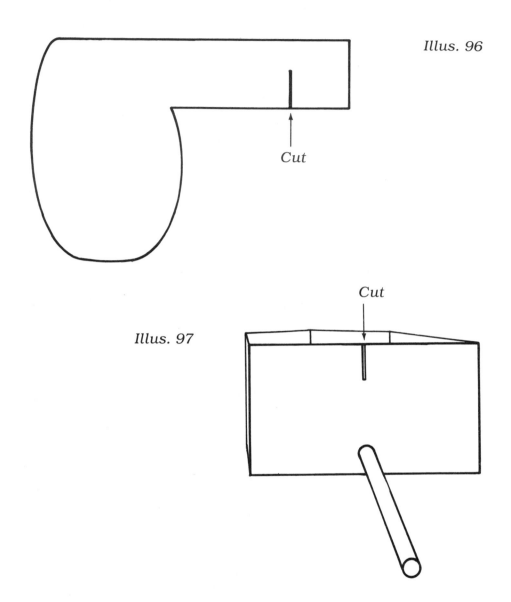

Illus. 96

Cut

Cut

Illus. 97

The cut shown by the arrow in Illus. 96 fits into the cut in Illus. 97 at the boat's stern. Just slip the rudder's end over the stern and interlock the two cuts; then set the rudder for straight ahead or for a turn. A bit of tape will help hold the rudder if it wants to turn on its own.

Try two cups for water power. You can make a twin-hulled craft (called a catamaran) by fastening two cartons together side by side, with each hull holding one or two cups for water power.

Whirler

Make two paper balls, one twice as heavy as the other. To do this, make one ball from a full sheet of notebook or typing paper and the other from half a sheet. Wad the paper tightly into as round a ball as you can make, then wrap some tape around it to hold in place.

Now you need a 6-inch hollow tube. The center of a roll of toilet paper or a paper towel (though you may have to cut that) is perfect. For that matter, a 6-inch plastic drinking straw will work just fine. A piece of string about 2 feet long is all you need to get the show on the road.

Thread the string through the tube so it hangs out at both ends. Tape the large ball to one end and the small ball to the other. Illus. 98 shows how things look.

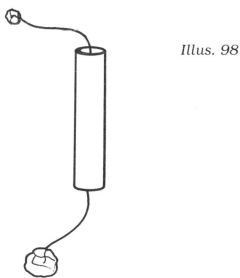

Illus. 98

Grasp the tube in one hand so the large ball is below the tube. Let the small ball hang out about 5 inches.

Now begin rotating the tube so the smaller ball spins in a circle around the tube. Rotate the tube faster and faster as in Illus. 99.

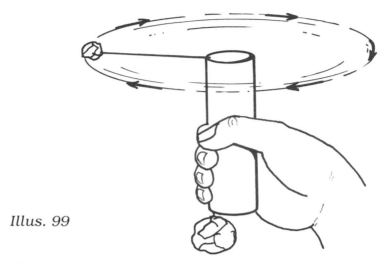

Illus. 99

Slowly the large ball will begin to rise as the small ball spins faster.

While you are spinning the tube and ball, slowly pull down on the large ball which, by now, has probably reached the bottom of the tube. Now what happens to the speed of the smaller ball?

Try making the light ball lighter and repeat the demonstration. Make both balls the same weight. How do weight changes affect speed and movement of the lower ball?

LAB NOTES

Centrifugal Force. Centrifugal force causes spinning objects to move towards the outside of a circle. This force acts on the spinning lighter ball to cause it to want to move in as large a circle as possible. The faster it spins, the greater the centrifugal force.

The relationship between the small and large balls is somewhat the same as between a planet and its moon (or moons). The gravitational pull of the larger planet holds the moon or moons in their proper orbit and keeps them rotating at the same speed, while the centrifugal force keeps them from crashing into each other. If something happened to allow a planet's moon to change its orbit, it would also change speed just as the smaller ball did.

Gyro Spinner

The Gyro Spinner is lots of fun because it surprises most people.

Cut a circle 9 or 10 inches in diameter from a sheet of cardboard. Cut out a 1-inch hole from its middle as in Illus. 100.

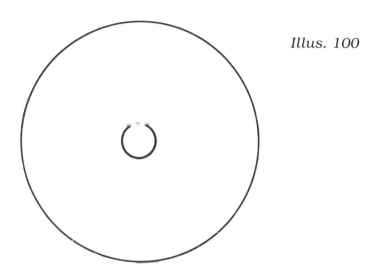

Illus. 100

Now you need a long wooden pencil (a round pencil is best). Insert the pencil through the hole in the middle of the gyro as in Illus. 101. With your free hand start the gyro spinning as fast as possible.

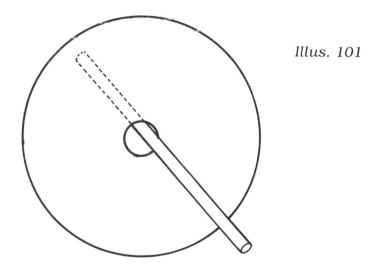

Illus. 101

As the gyro spins rapidly, begin tilting and tipping the pencil into different positions. Illus. 102 shows these positions.

Illus. 102

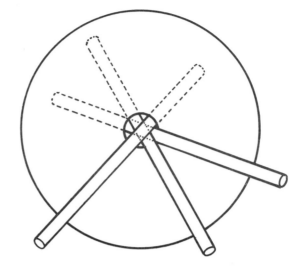

As long as the Gyro Spinner is turning rapidly it does not change position when the pencil tilts and shifts.

If you have problems with the gyro spinning its way off the end of the pencil, hold the pencil by its point so the eraser end sticks through the spinner; then cut a strip of cardboard 1 inch wide and 2 inches long. Attach it to the eraser with a thumb tack, and it will act as a stopper if the Gyro Spinner tries to jump off your pencil.

Of course, once the spinner hits the stopper it will slow its speed, so try to keep the spinner away from the end.

LAB NOTES

Gyroscopes. Gyroscopes are used as part of the guidance system of ships to help keep them on a steady course. Larger gyroscopes are used inside ships' hulls to keep the vessels from rolling during storms and when the waves are high.

The rapidly turning wheels on a bicycle act as gyroscopes as well. Their rapid spinning helps the rider balance and steadies the bicycle.

Balloon on a String

Just about everyone has blown up a balloon and then released it. As the air escapes the balloon sails around and around until it falls to the floor with all its air gone.

Cut an end off a drinking straw so you are left with about 6 or 7 inches of straw. (A same-sized tube of notebook paper works just as well. Roll it until it's about ¼-inch in diameter.) Tie one end of a long piece (about 20 feet) of string or thread to a chair or some other solid object. Thread the loose end of the string through the drinking straw or paper tube; then tie that end of the string to something solid, such as a table or chair leg.

Look at Illus. 103. See that the string runs uphill. Start your balloon at the lower end of the string so it travels uphill.

Illus. 103

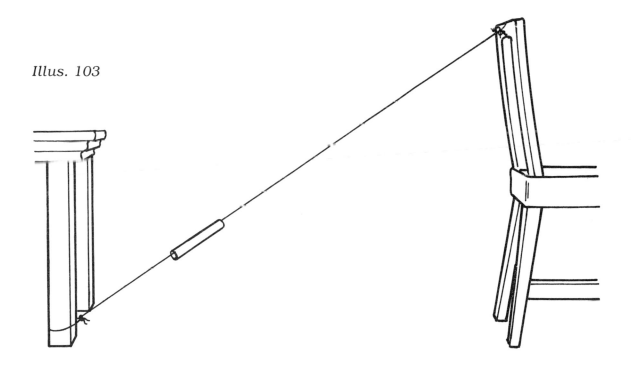

To attach the balloon, use two strips of tape, each about 4 inches long. A long, cylinder type balloon may be easier to use than the round balloon, though there is nothing wrong with using a round one.

Illus. 104 shows how to tape the balloon to the straw, but first, blow up the balloon. Don't press the tape onto the balloon unless it is inflated! If you tape it before blowing it up, the balloon is either impossible to inflate or the tape will pull off. Don't let the tape touch the string.

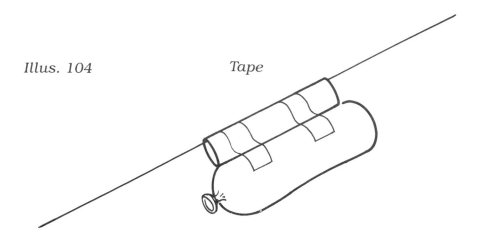

Illus. 104   *Tape*

Once the balloon is inflated, release it and watch it go flying up the string!

Try for distance records. Have two strings side by side and hold balloon races. See whether balloons travel farther and faster along thread or along strings. See whether the length of the straw makes any difference.

LAB NOTES

Air Power. When the air rushes from the balloon's mouth, the escaping air causes the balloon to move forward. The forward motion is in reaction to the escaping air.

Oat Box Surprise

Begin (obviously) with a round oat box. Carefully poke two holes in the bottom and the top, just large enough to put a rubber band through. Make the holes about ¾-inch apart. Illus. 105 gives an end view of the situation.

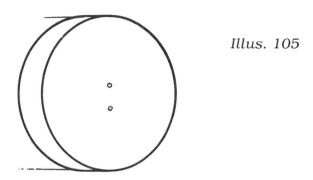

Next, you need a couple of rubber bands (if you have one long rubber band that's great, but who has a long rubber band when they need one?). Cut one side of the rubber band and poke the two ends through the holes in the bottom of the box. If you have two smaller rubber bands, cut both of them and tie the end of one to the end of the other. Poke the remaining loose ends through the holes in the bottom of the box.

Now comes the fun. Stretch the rubber band up through the carton, and poke the loose ends through the holes in the lid. Illus. 106 shows how things are going. Once the loose ends are through the holes in the lid, tie the ends of the rubber band firmly together. A pencil point, or small screwdriver, may help the rubber band go through a fairly small hole.

Illus. 106

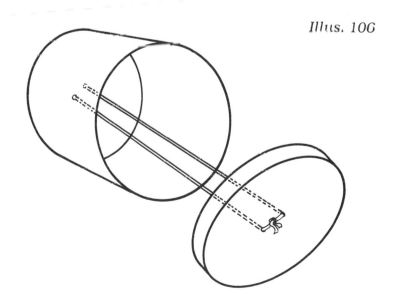

91

Now fasten a fairly heavy weight to one of the rubber bands inside the carton. A big metal nut is great. So are several metal nuts or washers, or a large lead fishing sinker.

Tie the weight to one of the two rubber bands with a piece of string or a chunk of thin wire. Illus. 107 shows the weight in place. Slip the lid on tightly, and we're ready for action.

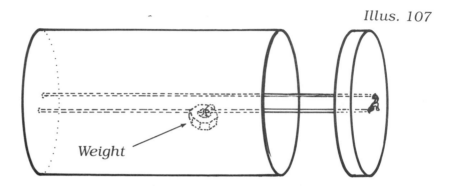

Illus. 107

Weight

Roll the carton away from you along a smooth surface. Give the carton a good push so it rolls 8 or 10 feet. It should begin to slow down as it gets farther from you. But then, if all goes as planned, it will come to a halt, and after just a second the carton should reverse and come back towards you!

LAB NOTES

Momentum. The weight is heavy enough that it does not turn with the carton. This causes the rubber bands to begin to twist about one another. When the carton runs out of momentum (the force you gave it when you rolled it away from you) it will halt. Then, if it has rolled far enough to have twisted the rubber bands fairly tight, the bands will begin to unwind.

Naturally, the carton rolls in reverse when the rubber bands untwist inside it.

Rolling Oats

This tricky toy will puzzle your friends.

You'll need two oat cartons the same size. Round salt cartons will work but the larger oat cartons are easier to work with and usually roll better.

Tape two weights inside each carton. Large metal nuts make the best weights, and lead fishing weights also work well. In one carton tape the weights across from each other as in Illus. 108. Position them halfway between the top and the bottom and make sure they are exactly opposite each other.

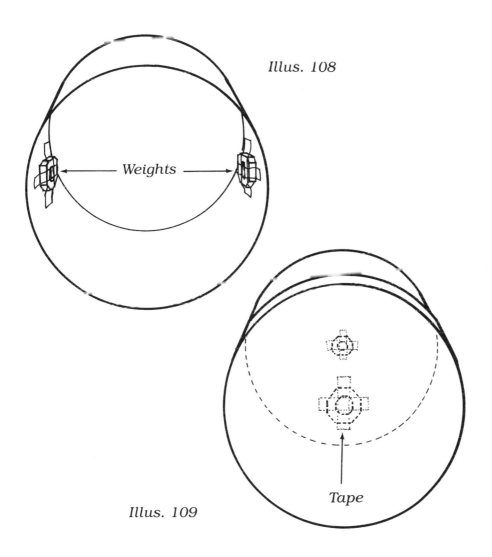

Illus. 108

Weights

Illus. 109

Tape

Tape the weights inside the lid and the bottom of the second carton as in Illus. 109.

Once the weights are in place and the lids are on the cartons, you are ready to roll.

You will need a ramp. A sheet of cardboard from the side of a large packing box is ideal. Place one end on a footstool and the other on the floor. Release both cartons at the same time and see which reaches the floor first.

After you have done this a time or two, challenge a friend. Of course you must make certain you have the carton with the weights in the center of the bottom and lid!

Roll the cartons along a smooth floor. Do they roll the same? Will the two cartons roll the same distance across a smooth floor at the bottom of the ramp even though one gets to the bottom first?

Try taping both weights side by side inside the carton as in Illus. 110. When you release this carton, you may be surprised that it will not roll at all. Instead, it will skid and slide to the bottom of the ramp.

Illus. 110

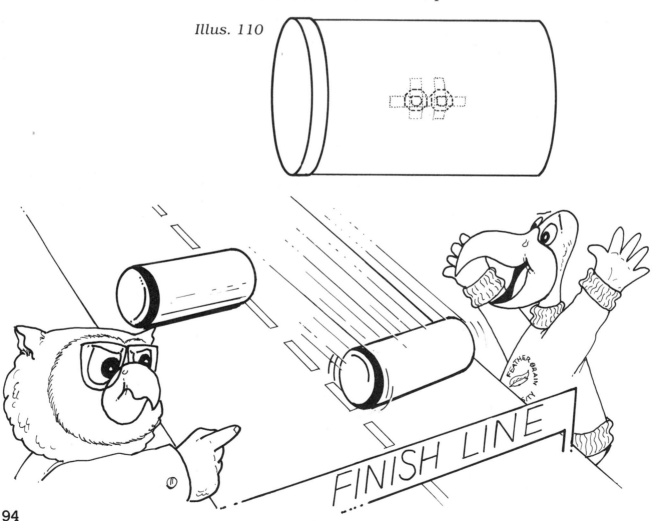

94

If you give this reluctant carton a bit of a shove to get it started, it may cooperate and roll down the ramp for you. Check its performance and you'll understand why the garage balances automobile tires so each part of the tire weighs the same as every other part of the tire.

LAB NOTES

Inertia. Inertia is a force that tends to keep things standing still, once they are still as well as keeping things moving, once they are moving. Thus, it takes a bit of effort to push a stalled automobile, but once it is rolling it requires much less force to keep it moving.

The two oat cartons weigh the same, but the one with the weights in the center of the lid and bottom starts rolling quicker than its mate. This is because the weights don't have to travel all the way around the circumference when the carton begins rolling. The weights in the end don't travel around the carton at all, since they are right in the center. We call this center the axis. The carton turns on its axis as it rolls.

Swinger

Take a couple of small soft drink cups and tape an 8-inch piece of string to each one as in Illus. 111. If you don't have soft drink cups it takes only a few seconds to make paper cones out of square pieces of paper.

Tape

Illus. 111

If you don't know how to turn a rectangular sheet of paper into a square, check out Illus. 112.

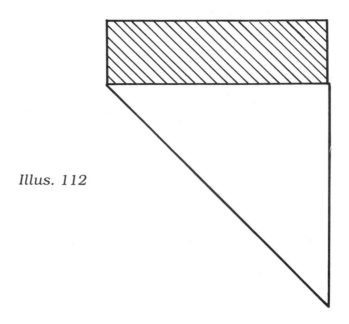

Illus. 112

Fold one corner over, and cut away the shaded part. When you unfold what is left, you have a square sheet of paper.

A 6-inch square is about right for the cone. Fold it diagonally so it looks like Illus. 113 (this should be easy since there's already a fold there).

Illus. 113

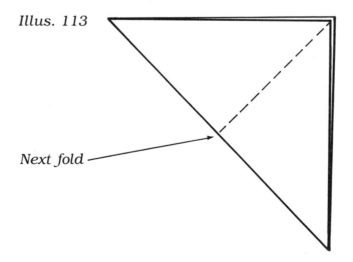

Next fold

Fold the paper again so it becomes a triangle half as large as it was after the first fold (along the dotted line in Illus. 113). It is now four layers thick. To make a cone, open the long edge of the triangle in Illus. 114 so three layers of paper are on one side and only one layer is on the other. Use a bit of tape to hold the three layers together.

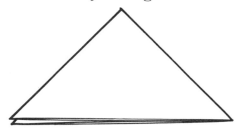

Illus. 114

Now tape the ends of an 8-inch piece of string to the sides of the cone. Illus. 115 shows your project.

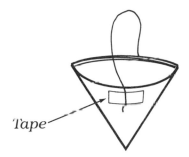

Tape

Illus. 115

Tie a 4-foot string to the backs of two chairs (or anything solid) as in Illus. 116. Cut two pieces of string 2 feet long and tie one end to the long string and the other to the string taped to the cone or cup, as in Illus. 116.

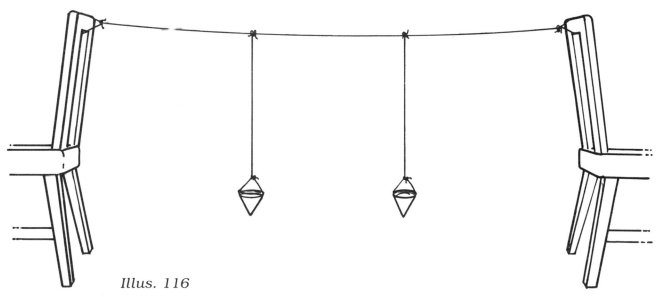

Illus. 116

Put exactly the same amount of weight in one cone or cup as in the other. Two metal nuts is fine. A couple of marbles in each cone is also great.

Pull one cone straight to the side and release it. Don't move the other cone at all. Watch and observe what happens.

Try adding more weight to the cones; then use less. Make one heavy and the other light. What happens if the heavy one is put in motion first? If you swing the light one first?

Tie just a metal nut to the end of each string. This will make a difference in how far and how long the weights swing.

LAB NOTES

Transfer of Force. The motion of the swinging weight begins to cause the cross string to move. That movement transfers to the string holding the non-swinging weight. Within a few swings of the swinging weight the non-swinging weight begins to move.

You can probably see that the two weights tend to swing in opposite directions as one acts as a counterbalance for the other.

As the transfer of force continues, the first weight will usually slow down and will swing less far than the weight it put into motion.

Wind Resistance. The paper cups or cones give the swinger a lot of wind resistance. This is because their large surface has to push considerable air aside as they swing back and forth. The smaller metal nuts don't have such a large surface so they don't use so much of their energy just moving through the air.

Three-Spout Pressure Gauge

A milk carton (either a quart or half-gallon size) is perfect for the Three-Spout Pressure Gauge.

Poke three holes about ⅛-inch across along one side of the carton. Illus. 117 shows how.

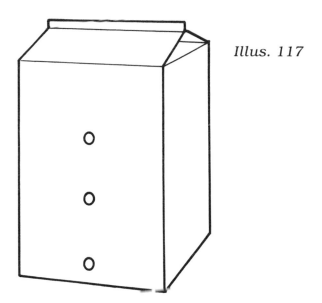

Illus. 117

Hold the punctured carton over the sink. Cover the three holes with your fingertip while you fill the carton with water. You can also stick a piece of tape over the holes if it's easier.

When the carton is full, pull off the tape or take your fingers away. Check the three water spouts as water flows from the holes (you are still holding the punctured carton over the sink, aren't you?).

Works fine for me!

Check the length of the streams of water. What is different about them? Repeat this demonstration just to be sure what you saw was not an accident.

Now enlarge the top hole a bit and try this project again. Does this make a difference? Try enlarging the middle hole. What happens to the streams of water? As the water level drops what happens to the water spouts? How do the streams compare with the original water spouts if you enlarge all three holes?

This demonstration toy is good when you want to show off to your friends. Ask them in advance to describe the streams of water when the three holes are equal in size.

Salt Patterns

In the later 1800's a French scientist named Lissajous discovered that vibrations could cause light rays to make a pattern. Not too many years later someone realized that a pendulum whose support moved would also make the same sort of pattern.

A pendulum is a string or cable with a weight at one end. The other end of the string is attached to something overhead. If you hold your plumb bob and let the weighted end swing freely back and forth, or in a circle, you have a pendulum.

For the patterns, we need a two-way pendulum or one with a moving support.

Cut a piece of string about 3 feet long. Tie both ends to the backs of two chairs and move the chairs so the string has a bit of sag in the middle. Illus. 118 shows this.

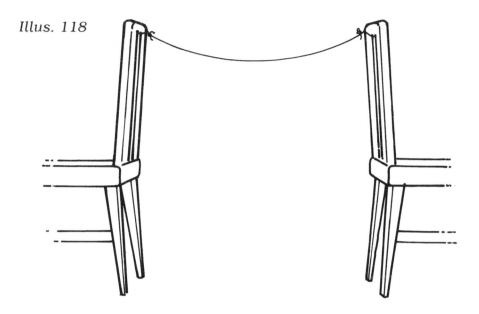

Next, you need a cone for the end of your pendulum. A water cup is perfect, but you could also make one out of paper. Use a paper 4 inches square.

Tape a 6-inch piece of string to the open sides of the cone to form a handle. Illus. 119 shows the handle in place.

Illus. 119

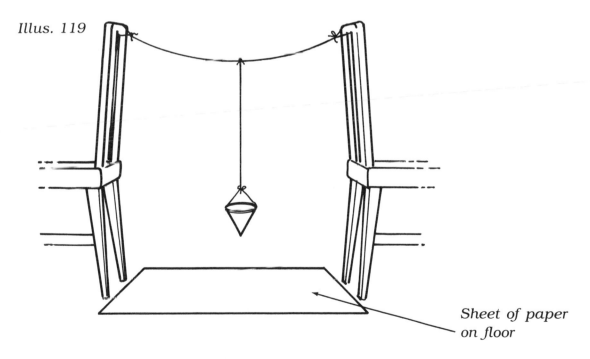

Sheet of paper on floor

Cut a second piece of string about 3 feet long. Tie one end to the sag in the string, and tie the other end to the string handle on your cone. This is also in Illus. 119.

Now place a large piece of paper beneath the pendulum. It should extend out as much as 2 feet in all directions. (You may have to lift the chair legs to slip the edge of the paper beneath them.) Dark paper is best if you have it. The comic section of a newspaper will work well.

Cut a small hole, say about ⅛-inch across, in the bottom tip of the cone. Fill the cone about halfway with salt. Hold the hole shut while you pull the cone back; then release it to set the pendulum swinging.

If all goes well your swinging pendulum will begin to move in a series of curves. In fact, you can encourage this by letting the pendulum go from a corner of the paper rather than from one side. When the pendulum either stops swinging or runs out of salt, you should have a design made up of a fancy set of curves.

If the salt does not run fast enough, just make the hole a bit bigger for the next run. If it flows too rapidly, seal the hole a bit with a piece of tape.

Don't use fresh salt for each pendulum swing. Just pour the salt from the first project back into the cone. Also, don't return the salt from this project to the salt shaker or to its original container. You can reuse the salt to make a curved design but when you are finished, throw the salt away.

By changing the amount of sag in the overhead string, your pendulum will form different curves as it swings.

Don't get discouraged if it does not perform well the first time or two. Work with the opening in the cone until the salt stream is right; then give your pendulum a nice, even swing and it should work well for you.

· 7 ·
Air Pressure

Free Fall Spinner

Cut an 8-inch circle from a piece of manila folder or the side of a cereal box. Hold it in the palm of your hand so the spinner is parallel to the floor. Drop it and observe what happens. Not very exciting, is it!

Now cut six slits in your spinner as in Illus. 120. Try to space them evenly. Each of these cuts should be about 2½ inches long.

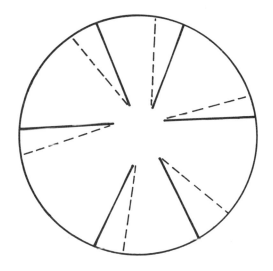

Illus. 120

The dotted lines in Illus. 120 indicate where you are to fold the material upwards. This folding creates six raised sections which will react to the air as the spinner goes into free fall. Illus. 121 gives a side view.

Illus. 121

Now hold the Free Fall Spinner up and release it. It should reward your efforts by revolving as it falls towards the floor.

Fold the raised edges at a different angle and drop the spinner again. Change the angle again and try the spinner once more.

Make the flaps larger by refolding them farther back along the material. Illus. 122 shows the old and the new folds.

Illus. 122

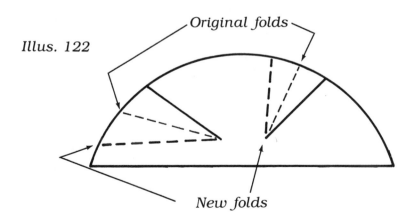

Hold the spinner higher from the ground. Fold the flaps up or down. What effect do these have?

You can color a spinner before cutting and folding the flaps to give it a brighter look. If you color lines out from the center, the spinner makes a quick twist of color as it nears the floor.

Falling Twirler

Begin with a piece of notebook paper 3 inches wide and 8 inches long. Fold it into thirds along the two dotted lines as in Illus. 123. The folder paper is now three layers thick and looks like Illus. 124. The dotted line shows the next fold.

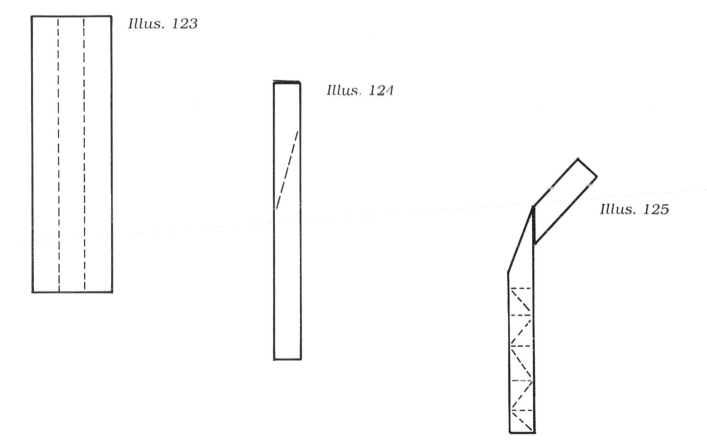

Illus. 123

Illus. 124

Illus. 125

The dotted lines in Illus. 125 show the next folds to make. Begin at the bottom and you won't have any problems. Fold the bottom corner up to make a little triangle.

Now fold that little triangle over to form a thicker triangle. Keep on folding the triangle over until your twirler looks like Illus. 126. Use a bit of tape or glue to hold things together.

Illus. 126

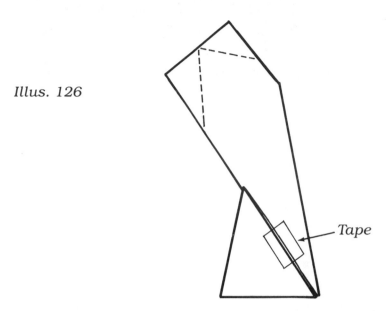

Tape

The dotted lines at the top of the twirler in Illus. 126 show your final folds. Fold one corner up along its dotted line and fold the other corner down. The finished Falling Twirler is shown in Illus. 127.

Illus. 127

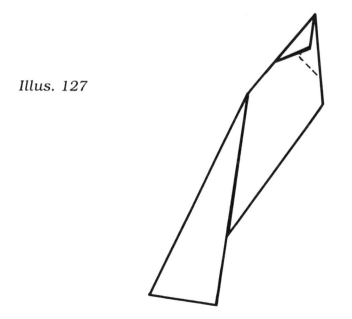

Take it outside and throw it high into the air. It should come twirling down, spinning fairly rapidly. You can adjust the corners you just folded to change the twirler's spinning speed.

Experiment with larger or smaller corners and with the angle of the fold. The higher you toss the twirler the faster it will twirl on its way to the ground.

Tumbler

Cut a sheet of notebook paper into a square. Turn the paper so one corner points toward you. Illus. 128 shows how. Be sure the fold you made forming the square is in the same position as in the drawing.

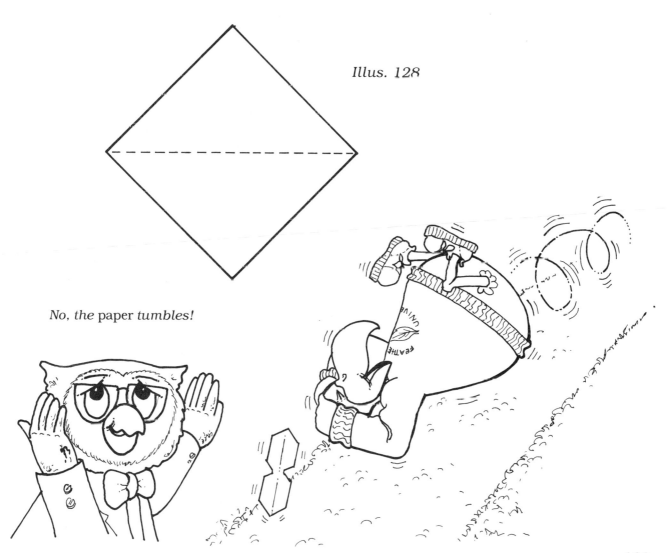

Illus. 128

No, the paper tumbles!

Now fold both the top corner and the bottom corner to the middle fold as in Illus. 129. Make these folds again as in Illus. 130.

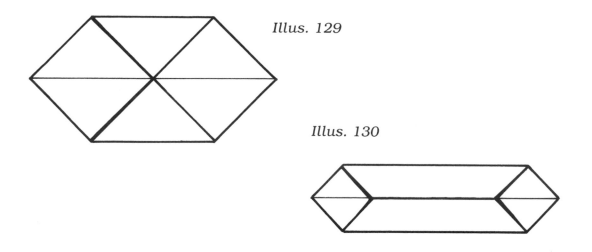

Illus. 129

Illus. 130

Pick up the paper and push in on the center fold so you have a little ridge right down the middle of the project. To keep this ridge in place, use two bits of tape to pull the folded sides together. Illus. 131 shows where to put them.

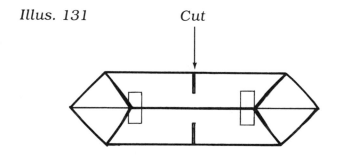

Illus. 131   Cut

Make the two cuts shown in Illus. 131. These cuts need to be ¾-inch long and exactly halfway between the tips of the Tumbler. An easy way to find the halfway point (if you don't have a ruler handy) between the tips of the project is to bend (don't fold) the tips up until they touch each other.

110

Fold the four little triangles of paper as in Illus. 132. A bit of tape or glue will hold them flat against the Tumbler. Turn it over so the side with the tape is towards the floor.

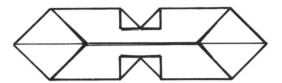

Hold the Tumbler between your finger and thumb as in Illus. 133. Now give it a little push and let it go on its first test flight. It should travel forward while tumbling side over side as it falls to earth.

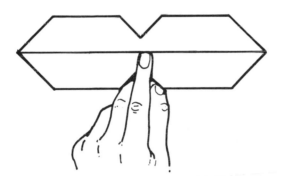

Illus. 133

Test the Tumbler to get the most distance out of it (it never travels very far since it spends all its time and energy tumbling). Try folding both tips up as in Illus. 134. Now test your Tumbler again. Notice that it now seems willing to travel in a fairly straight path as it tumbles over and over while losing altitude. Obviously, folding the wing tips up helped give the Tumbler a straighter, more stable flight path.

Illus. 134

The Tumbler is very sensitive to air currents. When it finds even a small air current to ride with, its flying distance improves a great deal, but if it is launched into an air current, it usually has an extremely short flight.

LAB NOTES

Control Surfaces. The upwards folding of the wing tips gave the Tumbler what we know as control surfaces. On an aircraft the control surfaces are the moveable portions of wing and tail sections that enable the pilot to direct the path of the airplane.

Since these upwards wing tips give a more stable flight, it is no surprise that they are known as stabilizers.

Wind Vane

We often hear people refer to a wind vane as a weather vane. This is probably because wind is so much a part of our weather.

For our Wind Vane you need a sheet of fairly stiff cardboard or cereal box material (you may have to use several layers to make the wind vane work well). Cut your Wind Vane so it looks like Illus. 135. It should be between 12 and 18 inches long. Be sure the tail of your Wind Vane is wider than its point—this is very important.

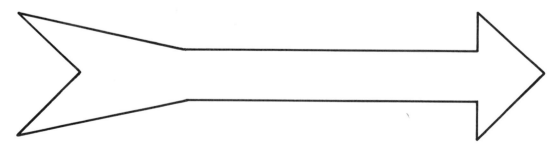

Illus. 135

Lay the wind vane flat across a pencil and move it back and forth until it is perfectly balanced. Illus. 136 should give you the idea. Don't worry if you can't get the wind vane to balance perfectly. You can tell when there is as much weight at one end of the vane as there is at the other even if it is stubborn and won't balance exactly.

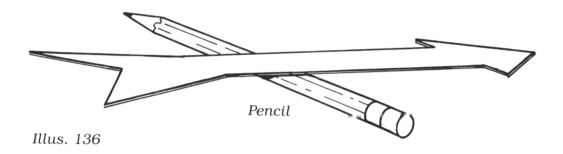

Pencil

Illus. 136

Make two holes right at the point the wind vane balances. These should be about ½-inch in from the sides of the vane. Check their locations in Illus. 137.

Illus. 137

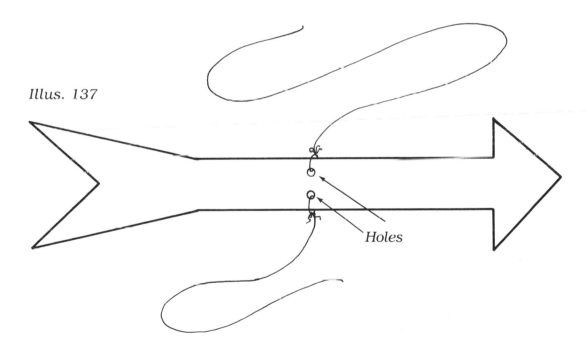

Holes

Cut two pieces of fairly heavy string, one 18 inches long and the other 12 inches long. Tie the longer string into the top hole and the shorter piece of string into the bottom hole as in Illus. 137.

113

Tie a weight to the bottom string (a large nut or bolt is perfect). Tie the top string to a low tree limb or any other overhead pipe or pole. You can even mount it to the top rail of a porch deck provided the house does not block the wind too much.

Remember, when using your Wind Vane, it points into the wind!

Don't use too strong a wind!

LAB NOTES

Wind workings. The larger surface of the vane's tail provides more resistance to the wind, which causes the smaller point to turn into the wind.

Invincible Card

You are going to make an ordinary 4- × 6-inch file card become invincible (a 3- × 5-inch card will also do nicely, as will any stiff paper or lightweight cardboard). Fold the two ends of the card upwards along the dotted lines as in Illus. 138. Make these folds about 1 inch in from each end of the card (for a smaller card, make them about ¾-inch).

Illus. 138

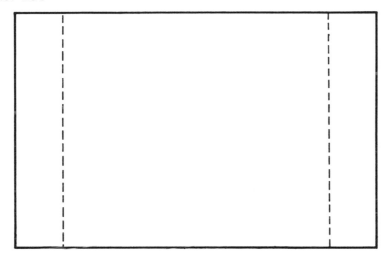

Now set the card near the edge of a table so the open side faces you. Illus. 139 shows this.

Blow directly into the opening. Try to blow hard enough to tip the card over.

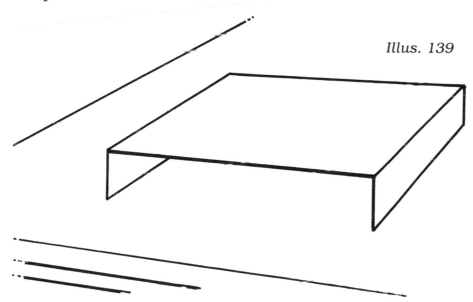

Illus. 139

After just a second or two you will begin to realize that so long as you blow into the opening, not only can't you tip the card over, you won't even cause it to move on the top of the table.

If you change directions and blow against one of the folded sides, the card is no longer invincible. It is easy to blow it all over the table top.

Use the invincible card as a challenge. Try it on your friends (just don't blow so hard you get dizzy!).

> ## LAB NOTES
>
> **Airspeed.** When air moves very fast the pressure exerted by the air is quite low. By the same token, when air moves slowly it creates greater pressure.
>
> The harder you blow the faster the air travels under the folded card. The faster the air moves the lower the pressure below the card. With the air pressing down at a normal pressure on the top of the card, and with you lowering the pressure under the card, there is no way it will tip over.

Stubborn Paper

Cut a sheet of fairly stiff typing or notebook paper so it is 7 inches wide and 11 inches long (don't throw away the narrow strip).

Place two books on a table or desk so there is about a 3-inch space between them. Lay the sheet of stubborn paper across the tops of the books so things look like Illus. 140.

Illus. 140

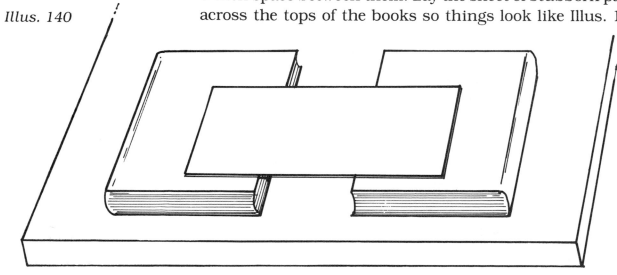

Blow into the space between the books. Can you blow the paper off the books? Can you even get it to flutter?

This is another perfect contest. Challenge your friends to how many blows it takes them to move the paper.

It just doesn't work!

Air Flow Strip

Cut a strip of notebook paper 1½ inches wide and 11 inches long (the strip from the last project is perfect). Fold one end upwards 1 inch from the end.

Hold a pencil or pen in your hand, and hook the folded strip of paper across it so the fold holds the paper in place. Illus. 141 shows this.

Hold the pencil and strip of paper in front of your mouth. Blow across the paper so you are blowing over the top of the strip. As you blow harder the strip will begin to flutter and rise into the air.

Keep blowing and you should be able to cause the air flow strip to stand nearly horizontally out in front of your mouth.

This toy makes another great challenge. Tell someone, "I can make this rise by blowing on the top of it." It is so obviously impossible most people will take up your challenge.

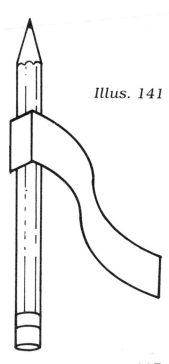

Illus. 141

Paper Wad in a Bottle

This one is sure to fool your friends!

Tear off a 7-inch square of paper and wad it into a tight ball. Place the wad just inside the neck of a bottle (about ½-inch in is good) lying on its side as in Illus. 142.) A bottle with a small mouth, such as a soft drink bottle, is perfect. Turn the bottle so the bottle's mouth points directly towards the "victim."

Illus. 142

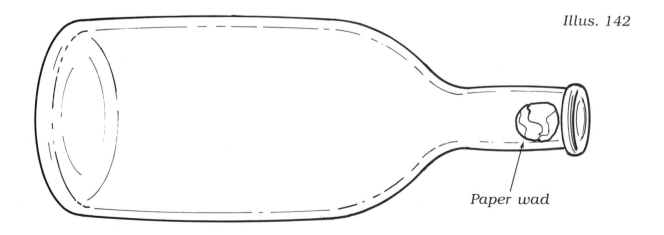

Paper wad

Tell your victim that to win the game, he must blow the paper wad all the way to the bottom of the bottle with one breath. If it does not reach the bottom in one puff, he loses, so he should blow as hard as he possibly can. When he does this, what happens to the paper wad will probably come as a bit of a surprise.

Any bottle with a small mouth will work if you don't have a soft drink bottle available. After surprising yourself when you blow hard on the wad, see what happens if you blow more softly.

LAB NOTES

Whirlwinds. The rush of air into the bottle creates a miniature whirlwind of air currents which force the paper wad out the mouth of the bottle. Blowing hard also compresses the air inside the bottle slightly. When the air returns to normal pressure it expands a bit which helps send the paper wad forward instead of deeper into the bottle.

Friendly Balloons

For this interesting demonstration you need two balloons. Round ones are best, though long balloons will work.

Blow up the two balloons so that each one is about 2½ inches across. Tie the ends so they won't lose air, and you're ready to set up this project.

Cut two pieces of string or thread, each about 2 feet long. Tie one end of each string to the end of a balloon; then, using short pieces of tape, fasten the free end of each string to a door frame as in Illus. 143. Position the taped ends of the strings so the balloons hang side by side with about 3 inches of space between them.

Illus. 143

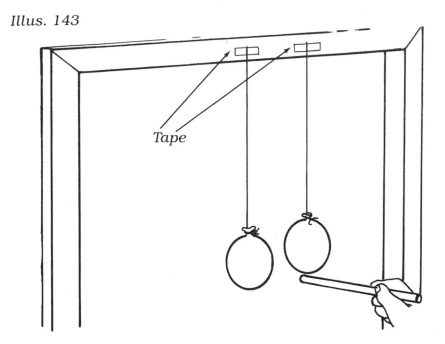

Tape

Now you need a drinking straw or a rolled-up sheet of notebook paper. Point the straw or tube at the space between the two balloons as in Illus. 143. Hold the end of the straw about 6 inches away from the balloons. Blow gently through the straw; then blow a bit harder. As the current of air flows between the balloons they will begin to move slightly. Instead of blowing away from each other as most people expect, they will come closer to each other.

Move the balloons farther apart and see what happens. Check to see how far you can place the straw's end from the balloons and still have the current of air influence them (just don't blow too hard or too long).

Now make the game a little harder. Remove the balloons from the ends of the strings and replace them with wads of paper (half a sheet of notebook paper wadded up is fine). Tape the balls to the strings.

Can you make these paper balls move towards one another? Adjust the distance between the balls a bit. You can move even these paper balls by blowing between them.

LAB NOTES

Pushing Air. You probably already realize the rapidly flowing stream of air creates a low pressure area, so the normal air pressure on either side of the balloons or paper balls pushes them into the area of lower pressure.

The Card and the Spool

Cut a 2-inch-square piece of file card or other stiff material (if it comes out as a rectangle instead of a square, don't worry). Stick a straight pin through the center of the card as in Illus. 144.

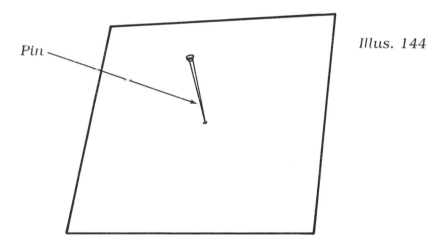

Pin

Illus. 144

Now find a spool. An empty spool is perfect, but you can use one with the thread still on it as long as the loose end of the thread is firmly in the little slot, which keeps it from unrolling.

Set the spool over the pin so the pin extends into the hollow center of the spool. Pick up the spool and card, holding the card against the spool with the tip of your finger, as in Illus. 145. Blow down into the open end of the spool.

Illus. 145

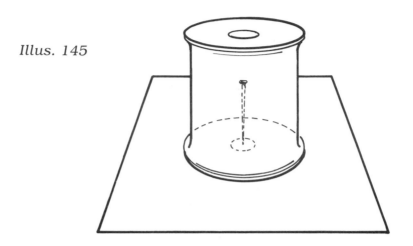

Slowly remove your finger, which was holding the card in place. If the card begins to fall away from the spool, blow harder. When you are blowing just hard enough, you can completely remove your finger from the card. It won't fall. Instead, it will cling to the bottom of the spool.

Try leaving the card on the table with the spool over the pin just as you arranged it before. Instead of picking up the spool and card, bend forward so you can blow into the spool while it is still on the table.

Slowly pick up the spool as you blow. Can you lift the card from the table without touching it?

Obviously, there is a low pressure area between the card and the spool. The normal air pressure against the bottom of the card does the rest.

Use this card and spool toy to baffle your friends. It's a great stunt, as you have already discovered.

Floating Table-Tennis Ball

For this toy you need a bendable drinking straw like the one in Illus. 146. Bend the end of the straw so it points upwards. Set a table-tennis ball on the open end of the straw. Begin to blow.

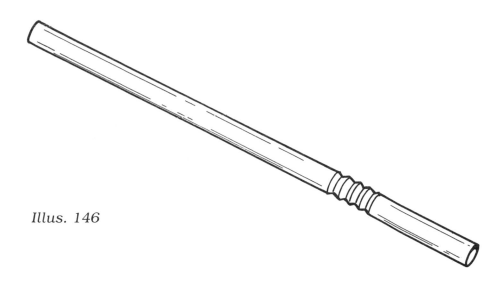

Illus. 146

The table-tennis ball will probably roll off the end of the straw onto the table. Pick it up, replace it on the end of the straw, and blow harder. You can even use the tip of a finger to steady the ball if that helps.

This tricky toy is difficult to make work because everything must be perfect, so don't get discouraged. Eventually, if you blow at exactly the proper speed, you should be able to do the trick shown in Illus. 147. When everything works perfectly, the rapidly moving air will be equal all the way around the table-tennis ball. The ball will hover in the air above the end of the straw, and you will amaze all those around you.

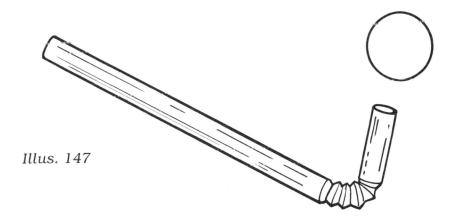

Illus. 147

For variety, try using a straight straw or hollow paper tube, holding it straight up in the air so you are looking up at the ceiling. Set the table-tennis ball on the tube's end and see if you can make the ball hover above you.

Pinwheel

Notebook paper is good for the pinwheel, but paper, which is lighter than notebook paper, is even better. Tissue paper is great.

Make an 8-inch square of paper. Draw the diagonals seen in Illus. 148. Cut along each diagonal from the corner about halfway towards the middle. Illus. 149 shows these cuts.

Illus. 148

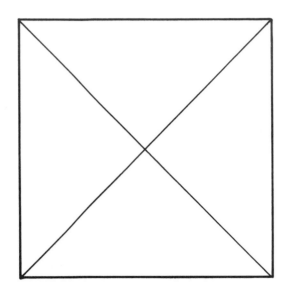

Illus. 149

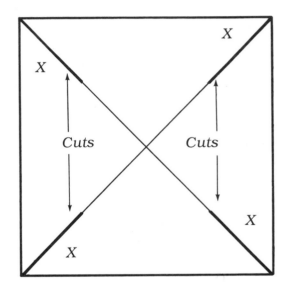

Bend the four points of paper in towards the center of the Pinwheel. These four points are marked with X's in Illus. 149. Don't fold the corners. You want them to form a curve as in Illus. 150. Place the tip of the first corner in the center of the paper and attach it with a tiny drop of glue. Continue around the Pinwheel until all four tips are glued to the one you just glued. It helps if you hold the glued tips down as you keep adding new bends and corners. That way you don't have to wait for the glue to completely dry before you bend down each new corner.

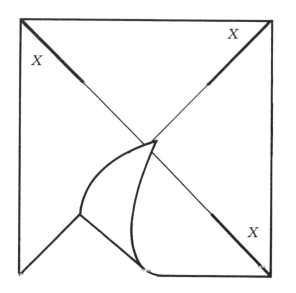

Once all four corners are bent into place your Pinwheel looks like Illus. 151.

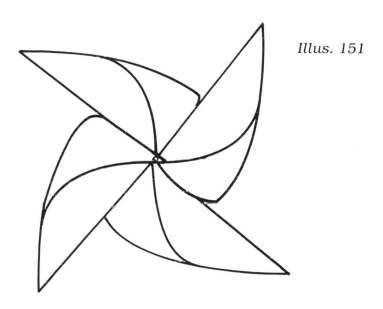

Illus. 151

Stick a straight pin through the center of the Pinwheel. It should pass through the four tips and the main part of the Pinwheel itself.

Mount your Pinwheel on a long pencil with an eraser. Just push the point of the pin into the eraser and your Pinwheel is ready to go. A plastic drinking straw or rolled-up sheet of notebook paper will work just as well, but make sure the pin goes through both sides.

Illus. 152 shows the rear view of your finished Pinwheel.

Illus. 152

Hold the bottom of the pencil or straw and swing the Pinwheel through the air. It will reward you with rapid spinning. Run with it if you wish; then try blowing on it. See how changing the air pressure will change the spin.

Index